THE A-Z
SPIRITUALISM
DICTIONARY

THE A-Z SPIRITUALISM DICTIONARY

PHILIP SOLOMON

Foreword by Professor Dr Hans Holzer
and Alexandra Holzer

APEX PUBLISHING LTD

Hardback first published in 2009, paperback first published in 2016 by

Apex Publishing Ltd

12A St. John's Road, Clacton on Sea, Essex, CO15 4BP, United Kingdom

www.apexpublishing.co.uk

British Library Cataloguing-in-Publication Data
A catalogue record for this book
is available from the British Library

ISBN: 978-1-78538-489-9

Typeset in 11.5pt Gill Sans MT

Production Manager: Chris Cowlin

Cover Design: Siobhan Smith

Printed and bound in Great Britain

Dedication:
This book is dedicated to my dear mother, Elsie, who taught me to be a true Spiritualist and medium. Her favourite quote I think helps us all:
'Death doth hide but not divide, they are but on God's other side'.

Authors Acknowledgments:
My wife, Kath, for research, typing and so much more. Chris Cowlin, at Apex Publishing Ltd, for a great job in publishing this book and a lot of other help along the way too. Libraries and librarians throughout the UK, far too many to mention singularly, but thanks to all of you.

Foreword

By Professor Dr Hans Holzer

Philip Solomon and I go way back and I always highly recommend anything he produces. It is always practical, sensible and professional. When Philip and I first connected some years ago, I had him over to America, and to be fair gave him quite a difficult time testing his abilities as a medium, but as soon as he spoke some special words that only others who knew me on the 'other side' could give him, I knew he was a genuine and incredibly gifted medium. He said things he could not have possibly known and therefore I was happy to endorse him and he gained my total respect.

This opened up the doors to our long and cherished friendship. He is one of the finest trance and clairvoyant mediums of our time and can be entirely trusted.

I am pleased to say he is now doing a lot of work with my daughter, they are going to make a great team and the A-Z of Spiritualism will be a great source of reference for their fans and also a very good source for anyone with an interest in the paranormal, the psychic world generally, Spiritualism and so much more, to quickly reference and have jargon that can be difficult to understand to the layperson, easily and quickly explained.

Foreword

By Alexandra Holzer

The first time I learned of Philip Solomon, I was both amazed and intimidated as most people my father (Dr. Hans Holzer) worked with were usually deceased. I read up on Philip and began to wonder if perhaps he and I should connect? Thankfully knowing of Philip throughout my home life and growing up, I was able to reconnect and rediscover what my father saw in him. Not only has Philip stayed true to The Holzer Family but has continued his work where a second generation of Holzers can be appreciative and continue to evolve.

When Philip asked me to do his foreword I was mixed with all levels of emotions. I knew I had to step up to the plate and position my paranormal bat for this request. I also knew a few lines just wouldn't cut the mustard. This request comes from an incredible soul for whom I truly believe as my father before me, is to continue to do great things in the field of the Paranormal and beyond.

In this ever changing field, we always need inspiration and positiveness to look toward when our souls encounter difficult moments on our life path. The A-Z of Spiritualism book filled with terms and meanings should be a vital part of anyone's library whether they work in this field or not. We are all one at the end of the day and what Philip has created is a universal place to come together and educate oneself for a higher empowerment in their own life. Knowledge truly is power and here in this well categorized and thought out book will one find such crucial information.

This book represents another important piece of literature in the field of science, spiritualism, growth, paranormal education and higher self-awareness. This is a tool and handbook for those who experience or study the paranormal and its methods to those learning for the first time. One can only benefit from such a dictionary in further enhancing their lives and the lives around them, living and deceased.

Introduction

By Philip Solomon

From my wide experience of people's requirements in the ever-expanding interest in Spiritualism, the psychic world and the field of the paranormal, it became my intention to write the book, The A–Z Of Spiritualism Dictionary. Such a dictionary is now required written in simple everyday language covering all the words used in every aspect of psychic philosophy and phenomena. It has become quite clear to me over the last few years the compilation of such a dictionary is greatly needed for the lay person to refer to.

Many people email me or write asking for an explanation of terms they are embarrassed to ask about, or find that those who are alleged to have knowledge in the subject are not really capable of explaining the correct meanings. I have always been a professional writer who has striven to express myself in plain, simple terms. Many of the terms and words presently used in Spiritualistic speech and literature need a wider explanation than is given by standard dictionaries. Terms common in the New Age movement in the fields of parapsychology and psychical research are still poorly explained in dictionary format to the layperson enquirer. I would now like to meet the challenge of researching, compiling and writing this book/dictionary for the large number of average men and women in the street who wish to understand an area that has been academically difficult or, at best, clouded in unfathomable jargon for far too long.

It seems clear to me that with all the interest today in Spiritualism as a serious religion, alongside the massive interest in mediumship that we have to admit has come to the fore through media mediums such as Derek Acorah, Colin Fry, John Edward, Sylvia Browne and perhaps most important of all, the media medium who brought this work to the masses through TV and theatre tours all over the world, Doris Stokes, people would need a dictionary to explain what some of the words they would come across meant, perhaps in their early visits to a Spiritualist church, reading books and hearing people talk about the subject area.

I have tried to put together an A–Z dictionary of many the words and phrases you are likely to come across. Of course it would be quite impossible to list them all. However, you should certainly find words that lead you to the answer to any question that you might come up with. I must also apologise for all the important historical people who have had to be missed out alongside some of the wonderful pioneers of Spiritualism and of course the many modern day mediums and workers for Spirit, some very well-known ones at that, but again unfortunately a book of this size makes it impossible to list everyone. However the mediums and workers I have chosen will give anyone new to Spiritualism a very wide overview of all the different activities that go on and the way that different mediums work.

I have also listed for you as many of the Spiritualist churches and other places that you could visit in numerous parts of the world. Again, I apologise for those that have been missed off the list, I thank you for your work too, but again it is impossible to list each and every one. Of course, many organisations regularly change their telephone numbers, even addresses and also have websites and email addresses. It also has to be remembered that various organisations come to an end and others start up all the time. All this additional information can be checked out very easily on a computer that has internet and search engine facilities.

I have also included quite a few words that probably fall into the realms of the psychic world, psychology, parapsychology and everyday life. They are important words, phrases and terms, because within the Spiritualist movement they are often spoken of and there are many who will probably ask the question 'what does that mean?' Hopefully this A-Z dictionary will now allow you to have understanding without the embarrassment of asking for an explanation of what at times can appear to be extremely academic or complex. This dictionary will explain them to you in a simple, straightforward manner.

A

Aberration - This simply means to deviate from the accepted or normal way of things.

Absent Healing - This is healing which is sent at a distance. A patient does not have to have direct contact with the healer and can be unaware they are being treated. The aim is to benefit the receiving individual, spiritually, mentally and physically. Spiritual healers are popular today and receive many emails and letters requesting healing for themselves and their family and friends. One of the most respected absent healers was Harry Edwards (see Harry Edwards).

Acorah, Derek - A practising medium from Southport, England. Derek shot to fame on Living TV, later becoming the undoubted star of the TV series Most Haunted. Psychic from a child, he also had a career as a sportsman, playing for one of England's most famous football teams, Liverpool. Derek's guide from the other side is known as Sam. He is also the author of numerous books, continually sells out theatres across the UK with his demonstrations of mediumship and psychic powers and in more recent years has become an internationally known star.

Additor - This is a Ouija-board that also has a small hollow box and pointer added. In the past it was believed psychic power would build up inside the box and would assist with prediction work.

Adept - A description of someone who has reached the highest standards of spiritual mastery of a psychic or spiritual pathway.

Adventist - One who has a belief that the second coming of Jesus Christ is certain to happen at some time in the future.

Affinities - Where two people considered soulmates are bound together throughout many lives, bonds which transcend death and reincarnation terms may mean eternally linked.

Agent - When considered in the psychic context someone or something who acts as the go-between in etherical communications.

Agnostic - A sceptic who dismisses any possibility of anyone being able to prove or disprove life outside of its material state.

Ahimsa - In the Hindu religion a term for totally opposed to, or non-violent.

Akashic Records - 'Akasha' is actually a Sanskrit word meaning sky or ether. The records are believed to be mystical knowledge that is recorded in the spirit world and to have a record of every single thing and life experience of every living person from the time of the world's beginning until evermore. You may like to think of this as a library and that the Akashic Records are a record of everything that has ever happened or will happen to us. Some very talented mediums and other psychics claim an ability to key into and examine these records. Some have described individuals' existences as being recorded in great leather-bound books, more modern seers as being recorded in digital formats such as is found on computers. One Chinese visionary known as Sujujin was claimed to have been able to access the Akashic Records and describe every minute detail of any individual's life history simply by being supplied with their name.

Aksakov, Alex - Early pioneer of research into psychic and Spiritualist matters, born in Russia in 1832, died in 1903. Claimed to be an advisor and counsellor to the Russian Tsars of his day.

Alchemy - The ability to turn base metal or elements into gold. Also seen today as spiritual in context - finding the inner and higher spiritual self.

Allegory - A story or description in which the characters and events symbolise some deeper underlying meaning.

All Saints' Day - 1st November.

All Souls' Day - 2nd November.

Alpha - The very first letter of the Greek alphabet. Spiritually the start of all things. The end would be omega, the last letter.

Altea, Rosemary - A worldwide renowned Spiritualist medium who heals too and has appeared on some very important TV shows, especially in the USA, such as Larry King Live and The

Oprah Winfrey Show. She is also a founder member of her own association of healers based in England but which offers healing to people worldwide. A published author, she has addresses in the United Kingdom and Vermont, USA.

Altruism - Having a wish to help others progress, giving of yourself to make a positive difference for others. A strong basis of Spiritualist doctrine.

American Institute for Psychic Research - Founded in New York city in 1906 with the remit to investigate and look into all areas of psychic and psychological research.

Amnesia - Loss of memory, often an experience many mediums have during and after trance mediumship.

Analgesia - An ability to control or not feel pain, an ability that some healers can exemplify.

Angel - In its simplest form a messenger of God. Beings that are said to come from the highest spiritual realms. Some Spiritualists consider them the highest of guides and controls, angelic in nature.

Angelical Stone - The stone that was used by Dr John Dee, psychic, medium and astrologer to Queen Elizabeth I. He used this stone for scrying and claimed it had been apported to him (see *Apports*), given by the angels Gabriel and Raphael. It is now in the possession of the British Museum.

Animal Magnetism - Words often described in the early days to describe an individual's inherent power and influence over others. Linked at times to the fields of hypnotism and hypnotherapy.

Animal Mutilation - An act sometimes claimed to have happened to animals killed with most unusual injuries often drained of blood with some suggesting they may be due to alien instances, ie, not of this world.

Animal PSI - Psychic or paranormal abilities recognised in some animals or pets.

Animal Survival - Many mediums claim that animals pass to the spirit world and are there to be enjoyed by people at their passing as the pets they were in this world or the animal creatures that were part of wildlife and nature. Some Spiritualists believe in what is know as group soul progression. That is that individual animals do not progress to the spirit world as humans do but can be part of collective spiritual progression, ie, many animal spirits may equal one human spirit.

Anima Mundi - Latin words that mean soul of the world. Early philosophers and today some Spiritualists believe there is an ultimate progression that embraces all energies of all life of all the universe.

Animism - The theory that all things have a living spirit or soul energy.

Anomalous Phenomena - Unusual experiences that cannot be explained away or answered by present knowledge of science.

Anthroposophy - The Anthroposophical Society was founded by Rudolph Steiner with the aim to raise men and women from self-centredness to higher natural awareness of the needs of others. A great emphasis is also placed on the importance and meaning of colour and rhythm and has been applied in many ways to understanding and clarity to conditions such as autism and associated behaviour patterns.

Apparition - A supernatural appearance which suggests either a ghost or spirit is viewable or present.

Apports - These are gifts that are claimed to manifest from the non-physical in our physical world. Such manifestations may be linked to telekinesis or teleportation. Often it is claimed a spirit, usually a loved one, has brought the gift to be given to someone in the séance room or other places. It may have special significance or sometimes of an unusual nature, such as crystals, small bottles of perfume, etc.

Aquarian Age - The Age of Aquarius was the supposed 2000 year period of enlightenment and love that would happen with the entry of the sun into the zodiac sign of Aquarius. Many astrologers suggested this would be a wonderful time but also many of them disagree on when it would happen suggesting dates as far back as 1904 to 2160 in the future. A popular term in the sixties when many interested in spiritual life were saying the year 2000 would be the time when perfect love and harmony would abound.

Arcana - Something which is hidden. Information and the

answer to secrets, mysteries, the future and the past, often spoken of in relation to Tarot Cards.

Archangel - An angel of the very highest order.

Aristotle (384-322BC) - Greek master of philosophy. The pupil of Plato and claimed teacher of Alexander the Great. Believed by many to be perhaps one of the greatest thinking persons of history. He wrote and commentated extensively on ethics, philosophy, metaphysics, spiritual matters, understanding and logic.

Arithmancy - To tell the future, divine, or guide yourself or others by the use of numbers.

Artefacts - Some psychics have an ability to use psychometry to date ancient objects or even suggest where they came from.

Asana - One of the higher or third stages of Yoga or bodily posture, assigned to develop strong positive thoughts on a particular situation. There are eighty-three other postures.

Ascendant - In astrology the ascendant is claimed to be a very important in drawing up horoscopes. In the simplest terms it is the degree of ecliptic longitude rising in the east at any particular time of night or day.

Ascension - Jesus being taken up into Heaven as seen by His Apostles. Important to Christian Spiritualists.

Aspects - In astrology numerous angles are claimed to mean good or harmonious reactions or of course the direct opposite between planets and other matters. It is basically an angular distance between the planets as they can be studied from our point of view on earth.

Asports - The direct opposite of Apports. This is where objects simply vanish from our world and are said to go to the spirit realms at the intention of mediums and others with psychic abilities to direct such objects away from them in this world.

ASPR - The American Society for Psychical Research - Founded in Boston in 1885, later being part of and incorporated into other organisations before being restored to its original title.

Astral - Generally the first word in descriptive form of the astral levels and other planes relevant to the spirit world, i.e. the first astral level.

Astral Body - Many Spiritualists and others with spiritual awareness will talk of an etheric double, i.e, that you have a physical and etheric body that are exactly the same.

Astral Light - The light that makes clear vision possible in the higher or astral spheres and allows mediums and others to see spirit beings, the spirit world and other things. It is the light of the spirit world as the sun is the light of our world.

Astral Overcoat - The idea that the etheric body at the time of passing over discards the inner body and it is the astral overcoat which contains the spirit that progresses to the higher life leaving the dead body behind.

Astral Plane - Quite simply synonymous and the same as the etheric plane, ie, the first level of existence in the spirit world.

Astral Projection - This happens for some people during sleep and is something they are unconscious of though some claim to be able to see, remember and control this state. A state of separation exists between the physical body in a bed and your etheric body which floats outside of it. Said to be linked by a silver cord.

Astral Sphere - See and read *Astral Plane*.

Astrology - An art form which tells of the character and life opportunities of individuals and groups, using extremely complex study of the planets, stars and their influence upon others. Perhaps not generally seen within Spiritualism as part of its doctrine but many astrologers are also Spiritualists and vice versa.

Atavism - The coming again of the personality and characteristics of your ancestors.

Atheism - He or she who has no belief in any god, deity or afterlife. An atheist could perhaps never really be a true Spiritualist.

Atlantis - An ancient civilisation that it is claimed to have been sunk beneath the Atlantic Ocean many thousands of years ago. It has an ancient source of support from Plato who talked of a people and great nation that was lost to this world in circ. 9500 BC. Many Spiritualist mediums claim to have had communication or received links that prove at one time Atlantis did exist. Edgar Cayce the famed 'sleeping prophet' is one such medium of great acclaim and respect within the Spiritualist movement of yesterday and today.

Atman - In the Hindu religion is descriptive of the great higher self. Associated also with Brahma, seen as the creator within that faith can also be relevant to an ability for an individual to split off into individual higher selves within that faith structure.

Atmosphere - Many mediums claim and others say they see and sense an unusual atmosphere, perhaps better described as the aura, that is part of and surrounds all living things.

At-onement - When a person feels at one with life, God, and as a Spiritualist, attuned and linking to Spirit, the Godhead, or Great Spirit.

Attraction, Law of - This can be simply explained where like attracts like, particularly on a spiritual level for those following psychic development and in their everyday lives.

Auditor - Within the Scientology religion an auditor can best be described in the simplest form as a therapist.

Augury - Another word for divination and prediction.

Aura - The energy field claimed to surround all living things. Some mediums and sensitives can see the aura usually in multi-coloured luminous bands that surround living bodies and can give an indication of health conditions and the feelings of human beings.

Automatic Drawing - This psychic or spiritual art was pioneered by Andre Masson. The technique was also applied to paintings such as in the work of Miro's paintings which were originally inspired drawings but developed into ultimate artwork in paint. Many Spiritualist mediums have specialised in such artwork such as Coral Polge.

Automatic Painting - Painting inspired from the spirit world through the hand of a physical artist in this world. (see Automatic Drawing).

Automatic Speaking - This is where speech or comment is offered without any conscious thought perhaps by a medium in trance. It is a fact that books, poetry, stories and other dialogue have been received with the claimed influence of the other world through automatic speaking, then generally written down or perhaps as is more often the case today, recorded on audio tape or in the digital format.

Automatic Writing - Written, typed, or word-processed work considered to be produced without the control of the conscious self. Automatic writing is a very old form of claimed inspiration from the spirit world to the physical hand of someone in this world. Word-processed documents inspired in this way is reasonably new.

Automatism - This is where the body and limbs are functioning but are not controlled by the will of the person. This can at times be either through the influence of a spirit guide or incarnate personality. It has been exemplified in automatic writing the playing of a musical instrument by those with no musical ability, psychic surgery, and other practises associated with the wider context of healing and Spiritualism.

Automatist - He or she who works through automatism but would be better described as working in the singular as an operator or therapist. See Automatism.

Autoscope - Any instrument, physical or perhaps mechanical in context, which produces audible or physical communication from the other world such as a trumpet, Ouija board, table knocking, etc.

Autoscopy - A word described by Feré to describe the vision some people claim they have seen of their own double. It can also be applicable to the ability for an individual to see their own internal organs and bones.

Autosuggestion - this is a word that describes negative or positive physical symptoms explained by the belief and thoughts of someone. A simpler explanation may be where you take a pill for a headache and the pain goes away before the pill really has time to kick in which maybe related to the placebo effect. The influence of the mind in the physical body for quite a time now and throughout history has been used in positive ways with regard to how a person feels about themselves or has confidence in themselves , this could apply physically or mentally.

Avatar - In the Hindu religion this is the word for the descent or alternatively rising up or incarnation of a deity in a human or creature form and has great relevance in the fields of the Hindu view of the truth of reincarnation which is accepted by some

Spiritualists today.

Awareness - Often described as understanding higher con-sciousness or the development or knowledge needed to understand Spiritualism. Meditation or sitting in circles of learning in Spiritualist churches is often undertook as the method of attaining psychic awareness.

B

Ba - Old Egyptian idea of a person's being, considered immortal.

Balfour, Earl - Famous student of psychical research, his sister married Professor Henry Sidgwick, first president of SPR, Earl Balfour was also president himself in 1894. He wrote important documents relevant to Psychical research, etc.

Banned Spirit - This is generally a term used to describe where a group of spirits work through one medium to produce collective evidence of the afterlife or to bring about other change in this world. The medium, his or herself usually links protected by a highly developed guide or what is known as the doorkeeper guide.

Banshee - In the Celtic communities particularly of Ireland and Scotland to see the spectre or a vision of a wailing woman who sometimes screams and whines as well, was often said to suggest a death in the family was imminent. Spiritualists do not accept this to be likely.

Baraduc, Hippolyte - Important psychic researcher of French origin claimed to be important by many by his work with thought photography. He claimed that a vapour leaves the human body at the time of death and could be photographed under the right conditions. The writer of several important books and other work he was also the inventor of the Biometer.

Barbanell, Maurice - 1902-1981. Founding editor of Psychic News, excellent writer of many books, a minister of the Spiritualist National Union, also at one time editor of Two Worlds, and one of the few authorities on Spiritualism to be highly acclaimed and received in Great Britain and the United States. He was also an incredibly gifted medium, one of the few to be chosen by Silver Birch considered one of the most credible spiritual guides and teachers residing in the spirit world to relate his words of wisdom and perhaps most importantly to write some books of great advice for Spiritualists then and now to guide their lives by.

Bard, Yolana - New York based psychic medium described by Professor Hans Holzer as America's greatest modern medium. Based for over twenty-five years in Manhattan, Yolana was the psychic to the stars. Shortly after writing her autobiography titled, Just one More Question, at the age of sixty-six, she passed to the spirit world in 2007.

Bardo - In Buddhism there is a state of awareness and existence believed to be between your last life and rebirth that is described by this word.

Barkel, Kathleen - British trance medium and healer, recognised and supported by the Spiritualist Association of Great Britain, given merit as being a very good healer, direct voice medium and a popular proponent of providing apports from the spirit world to those in this world.

Barrett, Sir William Fletcher - Professor of the Royal College of Dublin, acclaimed and respected investigator of the paranormal. Important in bringing British and American research groups together for the common good of Spiritualism and Psychic Research.

Bedbrook, David - A man who did a great deal of work for Spiritualism by association with the Society of Psychical Research and similar bodies and groups in France. He was considered an excellent medium himself and a fine lecturer. Bedbrook was multi-lingual and an author too.

Benediction - A short but generally formal prayer in thanks given at the end of many Spiritualist demonstrations and services, particularly the divine Sunday service in thanks to Spirit and God.

Bernstein, Morey - American writer and hypnotist who formulated a technique of hypnotic regression that is alleged to have produced clear evidence for the life of famed regression story, Bridie Murphy.

Best, Albert - Was a fine British medium considered one of the very best by many of his peers. Not only a fine demonstrating medium, Best is also credited with helping many other practising mediums of today in their early careers. So well revered that in 1994 he was given the title of Spiritualist of the Year and even dubbed King of the Mediums by Psychic Press chairman, Roy Stemman. An old school type of medium and very fine worker for Spiritualism and instrument for Spirit.

Bhagavadgita - Sacred Hindu writings that tell the stories of Vishnu and Krishna, a collection of teachings outlining the spiritual doctrine of Avatars and other gods.

Bhakti - Hindu practice for the support and maintenance of perfect balance and relationship with God and placed within the Bhagavadgita writings.

Billet Reading - An example of mediumship that was more popular in the United States than Great Britain. A gathered audience is generally required to write on small pieces of paper or billets questions or messages for their loved ones in Spirit. They are then passed to the medium or channel who attempts to answer or respond in a way that is acceptable to the questioner.

Bilocation - To be present in differing places at the same time. There are examples of such matters in all the great books such as the Bible and others and may be considered as part of and linking to astral projection in Spiritualism or a doppelganger experience.

Biofeedback - A word that describes a technique whereby an individual relates their feelings or psychological condition.

Bio-PK - The effects of psycho-kinetics on biological procedures.

Birth - A spirit entity is believed in Spiritualism to come into our world with a new birth and to leave the physical body at death.

Birth Stones - As related to the twelve signs of the zodiac each sign has a relevant stone which is as follows. Aries - Bloodstone. Taurus - Sapphire. Gemini - Chrysophrase. Cancer - Emerald. Leo - Crysalite. Virgo - Cornelian. Libra - Opal. Scorpio - Aquamarine. Sagittarius - Topaz. Capricorn - Ruby. Aquarius - Garnet. Pisces - Amethyst. Many younger Spiritualists find such stones of interest, especially those who are new to the religion or also interested in astrology

Black Art - Usually a term to describe evil practices, the opposite of White Magic as practised by white witches.

Black Hawk - Native American Indian controlling guide of British Medium Evan Powell, 1881-1958, fascinating because much research was undertaken that suggests Black Hawk's existence and eventual monument erected in memory in Illinois.

Black Magic - Practised by some witches and warlocks to hurt or harm others. The opposite of White Magic.

Blackmore, Susan - Born 1951. Graduated from Oxford University, England, later obtained a PhD in parapsychology from the University of Surrey. Blackmore became somewhat less in harmony with parapsychology when much of her work seemed to produce negative results particularly in specific areas where other parapsychologists had achieved what they call significant achievements. She has written several books and is linked closely with many organisations working in the field of parapsychology including the Committee For Scientific Investigation Of Claims Of The Paranormal (CSICOP).

Blake, Elizabeth - Famous American direct voice medium, extensively tested and supported by investigators of the day at the turn of the 20th century.

Blavatsky, Mimi Helene Petrova - Born Russia 1831 and one of the founders of the Theosophical Society. Considered an excellent medium some investigations suggested she was less than genuine, particularly those conducted by Dr Hodgson of the SPR. Blavatski continued with her work and produced a massive collection of material known as the secret doctrine which she claimed explained the ancient wisdoms of all paranormal or supernormal states and explained the wisdom of the East. She died in 1891 and is still considered an interesting character to read about and research to this day.

Blind - During some experiments psychics or mediums are not told of what an experiment will involve and blind matching is where information is not known by the examiner or the person being tested until the result is checked, usually set up by an independent person.

Blue - As a colour blue is often considered to have special meaning for those who can see such things in auras or in other earthly situations. Many consider the colour of healing generally to be balancing and healing in context.

Boddington, Harry - At one time held the post of vice-president of the Spiritualist National Union and has been credited with developing many mediums, psychics and healers. Boddington wrote many books and at one time built on the works of Dr Kilner's invention and practice of using Dicyanin screens for looking at auric visions. A popular book to this day is the University of Spiritualism.

Bodhi-Dharma - claimed by many to be the founder originator of Zen Buddhism in Japan and other countries which eventually developed into a branch of Mahayana Buddhism.

Bodhisattvas - The Buddhist idea of high beings having sacrificed their higher self towards Nirvana with the hope of eventual incarnation as saints through their altruism for men and women of this world.

Bond, Frederick Bligh - Conducted archaeological ecclesias-tic searches and research to find the lost buildings of the Glastonbury Abbey in Somerset. He wrote many books including respected opinions on automatic writing and was greatly involved in research and presentation of thought photography.

Book Of The Dead - These are the ancient Egyptian records and relics possibly put together as early as 2500 BC. They are set out in no particular form, rather being like a collection of chapters. Several versions of them are known and claimed to be original in context and can perhaps best be described as an explanation of how the human soul travels from the physical body to a higher life after death. The correct wording of them should read 'per em hru' which translated as best as possible in modern translation means 'coming forth by day'.

Book Tests - Are where tests are made to rule out the possibility of a medium using telepathy to give information, messages or be tested under strict laboratory conditions, for example when the medium answers a question he or she suggests a certain page of a pre-named book which has been made available to the examiner and relays several sentences from it which must be verified and accepted. Book tests were popular in the United States and are still used by some parapsy-chologists in appropriate test conditions and situations to prove genuine mediumship.

Borley Rectory and Church - The rectory and church at Borley, Suffolk, was claimed as the most haunted house in England, greatly investigated by Harry Price. The rectory burned down in 1939. The church remains.

Boursnell, Richard - Born 1822, died 1909, was a well known medium for spirit photography and at the time of his life a major protégé of W T Stead, a promoter of many aspects of Spiritualism at those times and some photographs received great acclaim and support from those involved in Spiritualism at the time.

Bradley H Denis - British writer and direct voice medium who teamed up with American George Valiantine who supported him greatly, yet later went to the media of the day and claimed that the work they had presented as being paranormal was not genuine and that communications from the other world were at best impracticable and most unlikely.

Braham Seer - The name taken by a gifted medium and seer Coinneach Odhar, a Scotsman born on the Isle of Lewis, who lived in Cromarty in the 17th century, claimed also to have second sight or the ability to see distant and future events and to have predicted that railways, canals, and many other inventions before they came into being. Claimed to be the medium or psychic of the Countess of Seaforth, it is claimed he gave her much advice that was incredibly accurate but perhaps some she didn't wish to hear, as eventually she had him put to death, burned alive in a barrel of tar!

Brahma - Hindu image in the verbal sense, most high god or great self.

Brahmana - The highest and claimed most spiritual of the Hindu caste.

Breathing - Many Spiritualists believe breathing must be developed and practised alongside mediumistic development.

British College of Psychic Science - Of which Sir Arthur Conan Doyle was its president at one time was credited with developing many excellent mediums. Important in its history were founders J Hewat McKenzie and his wife. It was closed down in 1920.

Brittain, Annie - British trance medium, close friend and one-time protégé of Sir Arthur Conan Doyle who considered her a highly gifted individual and was said to have kept an excellent record of her achievements and results.

Britten, Emily Hardinge (1823-1899) - Outstandingly gifted British medium and fine speaker and orator. She actually developed in the early part of her career with the famous American medium Ada Heyt. Hardinge is always credited with forewarning of the ship Pacific sinking and the very specific message she was given in trance from a crew member. She had spoken out and warned of the tragedy but is alleged to have been threatened with legal proceedings against her by high government officials. A truly great champion and major figure in older and modern Spiritualism and its development. She worked in many of the major cities of the world, brought into being and edited the famous Spiritualist paper Two Worlds, and wrote many books which are the corner stone of the way forward and way of life for many Spiritualists.

Brown, Robert - Practising British medium developed his abilities at the Spiritualist Association of Great Britain including tutorage from Ivy Northage and Gay Muir, and later joined a development class with Peter Close. Brown was one of the youngest mediums to teach development classes at the SAJB at the invite of Tom Johansson. He has become a well respected Spiritualist medium at home and abroad and also wrote and had published books about Spiritualism.

Brown, Rosemary - (1916-2001). Known as the musical medium she had very little real musical talent but claimed that through spirit influence she was inspired to write music in the style of Bach, Brahms, Chopin, Liszt, Rachmaninov, Beethoven, Schubert, and many others. She claimed she could see her spirit visitors and inspirers quite clearly and they would give her instruction sometimes even overshadowing her own hands so that she could compose and play the music much better. She wrote a most interesting autobiography called Immortals At My Elbow.

Brown, Dr William, FRCP - Harley Street physician and specialist and acclaimed authority on mental philosophy at

Oxford University. A major researcher of psychic phenomena and promoter of Rudi Schneider.

Browne, Sylvia - Born 1936. Sylvia Browne is a very well-known Spiritualist. She claims to be guided by her spirit guide Francine and came to major popularity through radio and TV show appearances such as the Art Bell Show, Montel Williams Show, Larry King, etc. Browne speaks of being on a mission from God to prove soul survival after death. She also founded the Gnostic Christian organisation known as Novus Spiritus, and has written a large amount of books many that have become best sellers. She has a popular hour-long show on Hay House Radio, talking about paranormal issues and offering psychic advice to those who contact the show. Sylvia Browne also has a son, Chris Dufresne who also operates as a psychic.

Buddha - The wise one who attained perfect wisdom and attunement in all things. The title Buddha can be referred as Gotama Prince Sakyamuni, who gave up position and family to dedicate his life to gaining higher wisdom. After great contemplation and meditation Buddha came forth with the philosophy of four noble truths which in simple translation may be considered The truth of suffering, What causes suffering, The sensation of suffering, and ultimately The path to the end of all suffering. Buddha today is of course the god figure in the Buddhist religion.

Buddhism - This religion is based on Gotama and may today have as many as 950 million followers, although it is impossible to put the correct figure for there are many who take parts of its religion or dip into the religion as part of their own religion and pathway. This may be applicable to some Spiritualists. In many ways Gotama may have been considered a reactionary rebel of the Hindu religion of which he was probably part, well over 500 years BC. Buddhism as simple as it may be translated in western terminology may be looking for the self (Atman), moderation and truthfulness. The Buddhist pathway and its eight avenues are said to be rightful views, rightful resolve, rightful speech, rightful conduct, rightful effort, rightful concentration, rightful livelihood and rightful mindfulness.

Bull, Dr Titus - American doctor and important member of the American association for the Advancement of Science. Bull worked alongside famous American medium and healer of the 1920s, known as Mrs Duke, to allegedly cure many individual and groups of patients with serious illnesses. In 1932 there was a published summary and outline of his conclusions relating over the last twenty years and also his suggestions for assisting spirits who have not made transition to the higher life, to be helped and his work is of interest and still used by some rescue mediums today.

Bull, Reverend Harry - Of Borley Rectory fame. Was one of the clergy greatly involved in the story of the haunting of Borley Rectory. Reverend Harry Bull, together with his family which included fourteen children, was said to be quite happy and in some ways promoting local stories of many ghosts and other paranormal activity taking place at the rectory and of a spectral nun seen in their home and the nearby Borley Church. Harry Price the famous ghost hunter greatly investigated Borley Rectory which has now become part of Spiritualism's history, yet one book, We Faked The Ghosts of Borley Rectory, by Louis Mayerling, who spent a lot of time at the property before it was destroyed by fire in 1938 gave a very clear outline that all the hauntings and alleged ghosts could be accounted for and they were not supernatural in context at all.

Cabbala - An ancient religious science which some link with Egypt but seems to be more appropriately placed as part of the Jewish religion. In it Rabbis interpret words and letters of the scriptures and numbers as part of the Jewish faith.

Cabinet - A box completely enclosed often with a curtain around it where mediums materialise spirits and other psychic energy with the claim that the space is required to build up the energies needed for such manifestations. Some materialisation mediums sit inside the cabinet, others do not.

Caddy, Eileen (1917-2006) - One of the original members of the Findhorn Foundation and spiritual community group. Eileen was awarded an MBE for her services to spiritual enquiry. Many people considered her a great inspiration to the Findhorn community and others involved in similar pathways. The author of 11 books on spiritual guidance received from what she described as the still, small voice within, Caddy believed everyone has their own source of inner wisdom that can be tapped into and taught others to believe likewise. Her best-known book was probably Opening Doors and her biography *Flight Into Freedom* was published in 1989.

Call - Word used to describe the response or answer given by a subject received in an ESP test usually involving the use of cards.

Camp Meetings - The best known camp meeting is held in Lily Dale, New York. Many mediums from all parts of America and other parts of the world attend and take part in events. Lily Dale in like a village made up of houses and residences all following the pathway of Spiritualism.

Candomble - A religion that is similar to the Spiritualist practices of the UK or USA, but is practised in Brazil. Not considered Spiritualism by those in the UK or the USA.

Card Guessing - Many mediums or psychics have been tested with cards such as ordinary playing cards and more professionally Zener Cards.

Carrington, Dr Hereward - Highly respected American researcher of paranormal and psychic matters and writer of numerous books on psychic subjects. Took part in tests with the famous Eileen Garrett, Irish-American medium.

Cartomancy - Usually describes someone who foretells the fortune of others using playing cards.

Catalepsy - A condition where the body becomes completely rigid and the individual is unable to move a muscle or limb. It can be something that comes and goes without warning and can last for varying lengths of time. Some experts in parapsychology feel it may be placed in the context of a temporary type of astral projection and it is the physical body that is seen in the cataleptic state with the spirit essence, although connected, perhaps nearby. It has also been induced by hypnotic states and during some cases of individuals receiving anaesthetics where perfect stillness of the body is required.

Cayce, Edgar (1877-1945) - Knowledge of the early career of Edgar Cayce might be described as sketchy, but it cannot be denied this was a man of incredible psychic and spiritual talents. He was often described as the sleeping prophet because during the sleep state he regularly diagnosed people's illnesses and conditions and prescribed or suggested the remedies that would alleviate or in some cases completely cure them. Today he is recognised as one of the USA's greatest psychics and a gentleman who brought healing and help to many thousands of US citizens and others from all over the globe.

Celestial - Heavenly in context, an adjective often used, e.g. the celestial planets.

Celestial Magic - There is an ancient belief that suggests the planets are controlled by elements in the spirit world who then indirectly cause the planets to influence men and women on earth.

Cerebral Anoxia - A medical condition sometimes used to

explain the experiences some people have in what some Spiritualists call near-death experiences.

Chakras - The centre of spiritual and psychic energy, found at points located on the human torso. Generally claimed to be in six main areas, though opinion differs. They start from the very bottom of the torso in the groin area and move up to the very top of the head. Some sensitives see them spinning and vibrating clairvoyantly and can decipher and suggest what condition or stage of spiritual development of the individual at that time. Some mediums and healers can also interact with and help stimulate change and balance in their own and others' physical body.

Chance - Things that happen randomly and cannot have a measurable predictable result.

Channelling - Some American mediums mix up channelling with what their British counterparts call mediumship, but generally in the US a channeller takes messages from disembodied entities not known to individuals or the groups, perhaps offering wisdom and philosophy rather than positive evidence of one continuing spirit being.

Charles, Keith - British practising medium who at one time had been a serving policeman. Keith described himself as a human telephone link between this world and the next and his police training had taught him to always look for hard evidence of a spirit's identity when communicating with them. Charles has worked with many celebrities and is a close friend of Derek Robinson. He also wrote a book that sold very well called The Psychic Detective. Very much a no-nonsense, down-to-earth man and a good worker for Spirit.

Charm - Many people wear small objects or talismans considered to bring luck or balance, as in a charm bracelet.

Chela - A term often used in yoga to describe the trainee or pupil, whom the master or Guru will develop and progress.

Chemical Phenomena - Sometimes smelt or experienced in the closed circle or perhaps at séances. Odours of ozone or lavender, electric lights that glow, yet remain cold and unexplainable production of liquid and sometimes fire have been reported.

Child Guides - Throughout the history of Spiritualism it seems that many young ones have chosen to come back from the other side and assist mediums and others as their guides. It is believed that some still have the child-like mannerisms they had from the years they spent on Earth, yet they are capable of offering extremely adult and sometimes academic guidance and can be extremely humorous and playful the way any child can be at times.

Chiromancy - This is the proper description for palmistry or of reading of the palms by divination of what the lines upon the hand means and also the shapes and forms of the palm and hands.

Christian Science - Came into being when it was founded by Mary Baker-Eddy around 1875. The religion puts forward the view that God and the mind and higher mentality is the only reality and that through the power of thought all physical ailments or disabilities are curable and in reality unreal. Spiritualists agree that thoughts are incredibly powerful and can heal at any distance and contrary to Christian science, strongly support, value and encourage traditional medicine, which should then be supported by spiritual healing and other alternative therapies.

Christian Spiritualists - There are some Spiritualists who have the same belief structure as Christians, that Jesus Christ was the son of god. They recognise him as the divine spiritual head of their churches. The services in Spiritualist churches tend to run along the lines of what happens in any other Christian church, except in the divine service evidence of survival after death demonstrations are the vital part of the service.

Christian Spiritualists - Belong to the Greater World Christian Spiritualists Association (GWCSA) formally known as the League, started by Winifred Moyes and through the wisdom of the spirit guide known as Zodiac. Christian Spiritualists make the declaration of belief and pledge the following: 1) I believe in one God who is love; 2) I accept the leadership of Jesus Christ; 3) I believe that God manifests through the illimitable power of the Holy Spirit; 4) I believe in the survival of the Human Soul and its individuality after physical death; 5) I believe in the communion with God, with his angelic ministers, and that with the soul functioning in conditions other than the Earth life; 6) I believe that all forms of life created by God intermingle, are interdependent and evolve until perfection is attained; 7) I believe in the perfect justice of the divine law as governing all life; 8) I believe that sins committed can only be rectified by the sinner himself or herself, through the redemptive power of Jesus Christ, by repentance and service to others; 9) I pledge I will at all times be guided in my thoughts, words and deeds by the teaching and example of Jesus Christ.

Christ Spirit - Generally linked with Jesus some Spiritualists hypothesise the view that the Messiah or Christ spirit has been part of many great teachers and prophets of spiritual wisdom in the past and may also influence and be present in some highly gifted and special mediums of today. This means the Christ-like essence does not belong to traditional Christianity alone.

Chupacabra - The Chupacabra or 'goat sucker' is an animal unknown to science which is believed to have killed animals in places like Puerto Rico and other Latin American countries by biting or ripping out areas of the neck. Some people have put forward the view that this may be an alien creature that has been left behind from a visitation from travellers from outer space or that it may even be an evil spirit, which explains why it has not as yet been caught. It has been suggested that it may be invisible to the human eye at times.

Cipher Test - This is a code or message left by someone before their death with the intention of proving they continue on the other side by repeating it to someone still living in this world.

Circle - Where a group of people sit together to develop in many ways but usually philosophically or mediumistically.

Circle Development - Many people today sit in development circles especially in Spiritualist churches with the hope of developing whatever psychic abilities they may have inherently or may find as they gain in wisdom. There are generally open circles where anyone can attend and closed circles, for the more advanced student and members of the church. Some circles sit for one particular type of development, perhaps clairvoyance, whereas other groups may sit for development of trance mediumship for perhaps one member of the circle. The ultimate progression is that members become working mediums, healers, or develop an ability to talk academically and correctly on the philosophy of all areas of Spiritualism. - Go on to list all the different type of circles.

Clairaudience - Extra-sensory ability most simply and best described as the medium hearing spirits, then passing on the messages from the other side to others in this world.

Clairsentience - This is where a sensitive person has the ability to sense conditions relevant to communicating with beings on the other side, with the aim of passing on messages that have meaning to those in this world. In simple terms this is a medium who senses things.

Clairvoyance - This simply means 'clear vision' and for a Spiritualist medium this is one who has the ability to see the spirit world and individual spirit people and describe them in detail for their loved ones in this world to recognise.

Clairvoyant Medium - A term many will hear in Spiritualist churches and other places, it simply means an individual who receives messages from the other side from spirits for people in this world without the requirement to enter into a trance state, for example simply standing at the front of the church or other building and working as an instrument for Spirit quite consciously.

Clairvoyant Paintings - Some beautiful paintings have been produced by psychic artists over the years, some in the style of the great masters of yesteryear. Others have the ability to paint a portrait of someone's loved one that is perfectly acceptable and recognised by them. This is an area that is known as psychic art.

Clayton, Arthur - Clayton was commonly known as the blind seer. Described as an English gentleman, fine speaker, and with good mediumistic ability he also dictated and wrote excellent books on the field of Spiritualism.

Closed Deck - A set of cards that are used for what are known as card guessing tests to test the ability of some psychics.

Coincidences - Many people have experiences of what they describe as coincidences. The only way they can be tested from 'by chance' experiences is by proper psychic research and many extra-sensory perception experiences set by parapsychologists and others tend to be based on this type of experiment.

Cold Reading - This describes a reading given by a medium to an individual of whom they have no prior knowledge or who they have never met before but in more modern times has been more inappropriately described as a reading where the medium gives a reading to someone whose body language gives them certain clues allowing them to give messages that could be applied to anyone. The magician and conjurer, James Randy, claims all mediums use such techniques.

Coleman, Arthur - British medium with materialisation ability. He was claimed to have the special gift of being able to materialise several spirit forms at the same time. There is a very good description of his work outlining such occurrences in Florence Marryat's book, There Is No Death.

Collective Apparition - Where a vision is seen at the same time by more than one individual.

Collective Unconsciousness - Carl Jung hypothesised the view that levels of unconscious thought and experiences may be shared by human beings.

Collins, Doris - Fine Spiritualist healer and medium. At one time vice president of the Union of Spiritualist Mediums, eventually renamed the Institute of Spiritualist Mediums. She had a worldwide reputation as a healer and also demonstrated mediumship not only at Spiritualist churches but in large theatres across the UK. She also had a major reputation abroad and was named by Professor Hans Holzer as one of the best healer mediums of her time.

Colours - Colours are the most incredible and often most unappreciated things of the physical and spiritual realm. Colour is all around us in this world but very often we miss the hundreds of more indirect shades that merge and make them up. Spiritually and particularly when someone looks at the human aura as in healing, by looking at that living energy field, much information is available to those sensitive to such visions mediumistically and in other ways. In a dictionary such as this only a very basic definition can be given for each colour and it is also important to remember that there are occasions when different people have seen different colours, especially in the auras, but the following is a reasonable example of what colours mean. Red exemplifies energy, strong character, a courageous physical person, but it can be a colour of temper and aggression. In healing red can be seen as the colour that is bringing in balance and burning illnesses out of an individual. Orange exemplifies how a person is relating to external influences and the world they live in, urges and wants, thought patterns that are progressive and a creative side. Yellow exemplifies spiritual and psychic abilities, intellect, but can sometimes suggest someone afraid to stand up for themselves, achieving spiritual progression and can suggest healing of the mind. Green exemplifies financial matters, prosperity, property, good fortune, and virility. It can sometimes be a colour of envy but is one of the most excellent healing colours suggesting balance, healing and well-being. Blue exemplifies psychic awareness, spiritual knowledge, intuition and sensitivity, inner balance. It is thought of as a colour of relaxation and calming, though sometimes may suggest stress or even depression when seen in a healing context. Indigo exemplifies developing psychic, even mediumistic ability, a seeker of higher wisdom. When looked at in the healing context it may suggest you need more relaxation time in your life. Purple exemplifies people who are both spiritual and very physical. Strong characters who like to lead others. When thought of in the healing context it is sometimes seen as benefitting psychological problems, perhaps even mental instability or stress, yet it is also seen in the aura of people with very developed mediumistic abilities. White exemplifies the colour of virginity, pure living and truth. It is also a colour that suggests someone highly protected who may have wisdom but may also be easily taken in by others. It is basically a good healing colour when given and also useful for those developing psychically. Gold exemplifies the colour of mediumship, of a strong healing person and sometimes suggests over-confidence but is also wonderfully progressive when given to those wishing to develop spiritually, psychically, even physically. Pink exemplifies love whether it is seen in an aura or given as a colour. It is a shade that will always bring the feel-good factor for those needing to learn to love, particularly themselves or give love spiritually or physically to others. Brown exemplifies common sense, middle of the road people, studiers and workers. When seen in the aura or given as a colour, it is very grounding in context. Black exemplifies mystery and often misunderstanding when seen in someone's aura and sometimes denotes imbalance and illness particularly of the mind. May even suggest a blockage that is stopping psychic or spiritual progress. Grey exemplifies illness and imbalance and is the colour seen by many to indicate places of negativity to others particularly in their auras and a colour that is rarely given in healing if ever at all. Silver exemplifies good fortune, luck and balance. It can also denote someone on the verge of breakthroughs in life, generally of a psychic or spiritual nature.

Communication - The word to describe a message from the spirit world to someone in our physical world.

Communicator - This is often the description given of a person from the other side to a medium to be passed on to an individual or others.

Compacts at Death - This is generally where an agreement is made between two or more people for effort to be made by the first to die to provide evidence through a medium or other means of their continued life on the other side. A very good example of this would be the agreement that was made between Harry Houdini and his wife Bess that whoever passed first would provide the other with an agreed code.

Complementary Medicine and Healing - Spiritualist healing is always offered, given and presented as a complementary therapy supportive to traditional methods of medicine as provided by doctors, hospitals and the medical profession. All other forms of alternative treatments should also be seen as supportive, never as a replacement therapy or course of action.

Conan Doyle, Sir Arthur (1858 -1930) - Wonderful man and pioneer of Spiritualism. The author who created Sherlock Holmes. Highly revered by Spiritualists to this day. Sir Arthur also had a great interest in fairies and was perhaps most well remembered for the so-called Cottingley Fairy Photographs taken by two young sisters, Elsie and Frances Griffiths, in 1917. Unfortunately, the girls admitted they had made up their story and faked the photographs and the press of the day brought great ridicule on Sir Arthur because of his endorsement of their pictures. Yet some media sources suggest the girls were persuaded to say the pictures were false and at the end of their lives, one at least, claimed again they were genuine.

Concentration - This is a meditative exercise where every effort is made for the mind to be focused very tightly on one focal point. This is hard to do and takes practice, but is considered a most important mental exercise for both the quieting of the conscious mind from everyday influences and to stop other psychic impressions coming in except exactly accurate messages or other work that must be focused upon by the medium.

Conditions - A word frequently referred to by Spiritualists which describes the present environment possibly affecting the medium's ability to link with the other side, such as noise and interruptions, though sometimes the word 'conditions' is used in relevance to specific conditions being set for a medium to be tested by a parapsychologist or other groups investigating paranormal phenomena.

Confederate - An American word that describes an individual who gives information they have found out about others to fraudulent mediums or channellers and other con artists.

Conjunction - In astrology a conjunction is simply described as the joining up of two celestial bodies and is considered an important link generally.

Conjuring - Many magicians such as Harry Houdini have claimed that through conjuring techniques they can replicate the work of the medium. Spiritualist totally refute this claim.

Conjuring Lodges - Some Native American Indians, particularly medicine men and those with the ability to link between the two worlds, would construct a special tepee or collection of similar residences.

Consciousness - The normal state of cognition which unfortunately can be considered detrimental to genuine paranormal activity. The medium who practices trance mediumship generally learns to remove him or herself from this state.

Contact Healing - This is generally in the Spiritualist church healing that is given at a certain time by contact between the hands of a Spiritualist healer and someone requiring healing who is present. Where contact does not take place and is done without the presence of the patient or receiver of balancing energies, this is known as absent healing or distant healing (see Absent or Distant Healing). Spiritualists believe that where the intention to heal is given it matters not whether the receiver is present or not. Healing is always received.

Contact Mind Reading - Some psychics claim an ability to read the thoughts of the conscious mind by holding their hands or touching in some other way.

Contemplation - A spiritual mental exercise where knowledge is obtained by focusing in a contemplative manner upon an object or person. A practice followed greatly by eastern religions and perhaps best witnessed and used where a psychic uses psychometry in his or her work.

Control - A control or controlled state is where a medium is taken over by a personality or spirit from the other side. The spirits are often allowed such control only by the medium's guides and usually only well-known personalities are allowed to take such control of any medium. The control can sometimes be a sort of expert who might be questioned or guidance to individuals or groups. It is generally the case that a medium in such control rarely has any knowledge of what they say or present and are really only the voice box for the spirit control. Native American Indians are often recorded as having being speakers through mediums to those in our world. They are considered to be people with great knowledge and spiritual advice to offer.

Control Circle - A development circle where the group sits for the development of usually one person. More often than not this is where a medium is found who has a very special, natural gift, or maybe has the potential of being a fine trance or physical medium.

Cook, Florence (1856-1904) - One of the most famous of materialisation mediums, in some ways considered controversial as some sceptics of the time regularly challenged her work, but she proved her abilities perfectly acceptably to Sir William

Crookes numerous times who always endorsed her as a most capable and genuine medium. She did a lot of work with Sir William Crookes and was claimed to be able to materialise the spirit known as Katie King.

Cooke, Grace - British trance medium and healer who together with her husband Ivan Cooke were the founder members of the White Eagle Lodge. Grace and Ivan are also greatly revered and looked back on with thanks by many Spiritualists of yesteryear through to today.

Cord, Silver - This is the cord that links an individual in the physical context and their etheric body. Spiritualists believe that once this cord severs then the spirit within the physical body travels to the spirit world and this is the end, or death (a word Spiritualists do not like to use) of the physical life of that particular person.

Corn Circles - For many years now quite elaborate patterns have been discovered in large wheat fields, and other crops. Some individuals claim they may be caused by UFOs, aliens or other intelligent beings from other worlds. Some still believe this even though many tricksters have actually shown the techniques they use to produce such crop circles.

Correlation - A word that describes a clear association made between two situations. For example correlation would have been considered to have taken place if a sitter was given the same message by two different mediums.

Cosmic Consciousness - When an individual finds they have reached the stage of knowledge of all life throughout the universe, some religious orders and groups say they have attained cosmic consciousness and that spiritual and intellectual progression has been gained.

Coulston, Charles - MSNU. Secretary of the Finance Committee and a very fine servant of Spiritualism.

Coulston, Lynette - MSNU. Chairman/Secretary of Spiritualist Aid. Fine instrument and worker for Spirit.

Coven - Meeting of witches and warlocks of various group sizes. A true coven consists of 13 individuals, six mixed couples and one who would have the role of high priest or priestess.

Crandon, Margery - Historically claimed to be one of the best

American mediums of her time, she was tested under quite strict conditions and was described as attaining excellent standards of mediumship, etc., with authorities of the time such as Dr Gustave Geley and Professor Richet testing her. Harry Price considered this fraudproof.

Cremation - To burn the final remains of a human being with fire. This method of disposal of human bodies still causes some controversy among Spiritualists and some claim that cremation may take place too early for the etheric or inner spirit to leave its earthly body and that some problems may be experienced before its eventual progression to the higher life takes place. However many have come back from the other side to say cremation has had no effect whatsoever on their passing over easily and comfortably to the other side.

Crisis Apparitions - There have been descriptions of apparitions appearing at moments of great crisis to individuals and groups, a perfect example being the Angels of Mons seen by the soldiers of the First World War. Later claimed to have been physical in context, many old soldiers continue to claim they were undoubtedly apparitions from the other side which in some situations guided them to safety and helped them avoid certain death.

Crookes, Sir William (1832-1919) - A wonderful and talented physicist of the nineteenth century who made important investigations of Spiritualism. He claimed in his early years that scientific methods of investigation would prove Spiritualism worthless and part only of other magic practices. However, after testing the likes of D. D. Home and also investigations of Florence Cook, he found himself in a position of supporting the truth of Spiritualism despite at that time being in great danger of ridicule from his contemporaries in the scientific world. Sir William is considered a great champion of Spiritualism in the past and revered by its members today.

Crop Circles - see Corn Circles.

Cross Correspondence - This is where differing information is given quite independently by more than one medium but when looked at collectively proved to be acceptable evidence of communication from someone on the other side.

Crowley, Edward Alexander - Known as Aleister. Born in the English Midlands in Leamington in 1875, died 1947. Perhaps the most famous occultist of them all. Titled himself as the Beast of the Apocalypse and named by the media as the wickedest man in the world. A person of terrible excesses, many claimed him to be one of the most outstanding occultists and magicians of modern times. An important member of the Hermetic order of the Golden Dawn, his thesis on life was that you could do anything you pleased without recount and although when his books are read it certainly suggests he could link with spirits and higher realms it was his intention to draw in the dark forces not the good. His life was the complete opposite of what a Spiritualist would strive for, but those interested in both sides of the coin of light and darkness in Spiritual context would be advised to read or study further Crowley's work. His books include *Magic In Theory and Practice*, published 1929, and his *The Book of Thoth* (1944).

Cryptesthesia - A word used in a descriptive context to explain a sixth sense. The theory is that paranormal ability is activated by an unknown external vibration, 'the vibrations of reality'. In some schools this is offered as an alternative explanation of spirit communication. Cryptesthesia would perhaps most easily be described today by the words extra-sensory perception.

Cryptomnesia - Means unconscious memory, that which is put on file if you like, but can be withdrawn and remembered under the right circumstances. A medium would best be described as using this in the same way an operator records information on the hard drive of a personal computer and makes it available when requested in the future. The medium does this from the unconscious mind perhaps in trance or in other stages of extremely deep meditative mediumship.

Crystal Gazing - One of the oldest methods of divination. Real crystal balls are made purely of crystal whereas many of the fortune tellers' orbs are probably made of crystal lead glass or simply just glass. It is said that the orb becomes cloud-like before symbols appear that can be interpreted by the reader. True Spiritualist mediums or developed clairvoyants do not require such an aid.

Culture Heroes - Individuals whose teachings have made them important people to read about or listen to. Culture heroes became a fashionable term amongst some members of the New Age movement. Perhaps at their very highest standards of attainment they may be considered to be of divine status, gurus or even prophets of sorts.

Cummins, Geraldine - An excellent Irish medium and revered for her work as an automatist. She is said to have written words, scripts and books, in well constructed form at amazing speeds and have told stories or perhaps more applicably, given reports of periods in history not yet known to this day. Her work has been examined by experts in the field of history and other academic standing who have verified it as being worthy of acceptance and further research. Cummins also undertook a collection of tests and experiments with revered physician Dr Connell of Ireland which resulted in Connell considering the possibility of the origin of some patients' maladies being accessible through their psychometrical experiments. He further claimed they would have to be considered as possible evidence for the truth of Karmic Law and reincarnation.

Curran, Mrs John H. - Fine American medium who wrote the collection of respected literary works for the Patience Worth book series revered by many Spiritualists in the past. Curran was not of an academic background, yet wrote in a most professional and high-quality manner and could speak when required with an eloquent tongue. Many considered her a most spirited and remarkably spiritually gifted person.

Curse - Where someone speaks of sending you a bad spell, hexing you, or generally wishing you ill (this can also be in the written form), it can be considered a curse. Gipsies were said to always curse individuals and groups who offended them in some way.

D

Daimôn - This was the name of the spirit guide that ancient philosophy suggests guided Socrates when he was in need of spiritual influence from the higher world.

Dalai Lama - The spiritual leader on Earth of Lamaism, believed to be a reincarnation of the all-knowing one. In simple terms, Bodhisattva, and generally chosen by Lamas from all over the world, sometimes the most ordinary of babies but whose time of birth astrologically suggests he is the chosen one.

Davenport Brothers - Ira and William, famed American mediums of the nineteenth century who gave many public demonstrations both sides of the Atlantic and France. Also escapologists whom no rope or secure fastenings could hold. Many believe they had paranormal assistance and they are claimed to have performed before royalty including the Russian Tsar and even Napoleon himself.

Davis, Andrew Jackson - The famous Poughkeepsie seer, 1826-1910. Excellent medium and author of many worthy books on Spiritualism. Born of unread parents and brought up in less than ideal circumstances for a future academic, Davis progressed as a clairvoyant and was already working thus before receiving any education, which he took up at the age of sixteen. Also skilled in hypnotism he eventually met Galen and Swedenborg and received tutorage academically and also spiritually. It wasn't long before that he was writing books and lecturing, often in the trance state, sometimes in English, sometimes in Hebrew. Some of his trance work in the Jewish language was highly acclaimed by Dr Busch, professor of ancient Egypt at the New York University. One of his best known publications was The Principles of Nature, Her Divine Revelations and a Voice to Mankind. He is a major figure in past and present Spiritualism.

Dead Sea Scrolls - Ancient documents of Jewish background, although specifically associated with the Essenes of which Jesus Christ has been claimed by many to have been a member, probably based at Qumran dating back perhaps to well over a hundred years before the life of Jesus, and towards the end of the first century. Parts of the scrolls have been found in varying conditions in caves from 1947 onwards and are mostly records of Old Testament documents and opinions, together with rules and life pathways for the Essenes themselves. The documents are fascinating to Christians and Spiritualists alike.

Death - To the Spiritualist, simply leaving behind the physical body. The spirit continues on, which some call the etheric body. The spirit moves on to the higher levels of the spirit world. Spiritualists believe that the personality and character of a person are not changed. Some Spiritualists believe there is no longer the need to eat, rest, or work in any way and that the sex life is not continued in couples, although some Spiritualists believe the spirit world is what you wish it to be and all the aforesaid are there for you should you wish them to be. The view is that the higher mind has the strength of power and action upon the spirit world to make it recognisable and perfect bliss, yet still with the pleasures of the earth world retained if that is what is important to you.

Death-Bed Experiences - Many people relate the experience of their loved ones perhaps reviving at the point of death even from the most extreme of debilitating conditions to say they can see and hear loved ones that have passed to the other side, often commenting that someone they know has come to take them to the other side. Some have had quite remarkable experiences, and even atheists have reported figures from the Bible and other great books appearing to them, to prove the existence of the higher life. To many Spiritualists this is completely understood and expected to be a fact at the time of their passing over that a loved one will come to take them to the spirit world.

Decline Effect - A reduced performance on a Psi test when the test is examined again after being repeated.

Deism - The understanding, belief and faith that there is but one

God as creator of everything.

Déjà Vu - When someone senses that a place they are at in the present or a repeating situation is relevant to somewhere they have been before, perhaps in another life.

Delphic Oracle - The famous ancient Greek oracle of the Greek prophetess Pythia, claimed to have spoken to people while in trance and surrounded by fire. The Greek writer and keeper of records, Plutarch, claimed she was an advisor to the ancient kings.

Delta - A word that describes any anomalous experience.

Delusion - An incorrect opinion, fallacy, or misinterpretation.

Dematerialisation - The appearance or disappearance, more appropriately of the materialised form. In séances of yesteryear it was a popular practice that efforts would be made for part of the medium's body to become invisible for a short time. The disappearance of objects to other places is also relevant here (see Apports).

Demon - A very evil spirit or entity.

Demonic Possession - Where a person is believed or claimed to be possessed by an evil entity or spirit.

Deport - To move an object paranormally, usually by dematerialising and then materialising it elsewhere.

Dermography - The appearance of or to physically wish for written text upon the skin.

Dervish - This is a member of a Muslim religious order who emphasises Spiritualism and mysticism within their religious and life pathways. Some priests are known for spinning around for long periods to attain higher states of consciousness (Whirling Dervishes).

Descendent - A degree of the ecliptic, which in astrological terms means being set opposite an individual ascendant.

Desmond, Shaw - Well-known speaker on Spiritualistic matters and also acclaimed Irish poet. Wrote several books around the 1940s and 50s which are considered worthy in Spiritualism. A Spiritualist who had a strong belief in reincarnation and past lives.

Determinism - The opposite of free will, which suggests that a human's position in life is the result of external influences on his or her will.

Deva - In its simplest Western context, a term in the Hindu religion for a god or godlike figure.

Devachan - A term in the Hindu religion for the state a person is in when they are between reincarnated lives.

Development, Mediumistic - Any person who wishes to become a medium really needs to join a Spiritualist church and in the early days join in the open circle, progress to a closed circle, and if at all possible find individuals who can help them progress towards becoming a medium.

Devil - The concept of 'the Devil' is not really recognised in Spiritualism, which rather suggests that all evil is the result of men or women's own inner cruelty or perhaps lack of altruism for others. The religion teaches that we have a responsibility for all we do wrong and are accountable for all good and bad done in this world, both here and on the higher levels of Spirit existence too. There are other names for the Devil such as Old Nick, Beelzebub, Lord of the Flies, Baphomet, Mephistopheles and Satan. In many ways all these names are descriptive of the complete embodiment of evil or wickedness particularly in the Christian religions and faiths.

Dharana - The sixth level of progression within Yoga said to be relevant to quietening and steadying of the mind.

Dharma - In the Buddhist religion the law of duty at any given time.

Dhyana - The seventh level of progression in Yoga with the emphasis on absolute focused ideas.

Diagnosis Healing - Some Spiritualist healers are said to have the ability to diagnose illness or imbalanced situations often alongside their hands-on healing spiritual skills. This is sometimes because some healers achieve the assistance of a physician or doctor from the spirit world. Emphasis is always placed on healing rather than diagnosis in the professional teaching of healers and pronounced diagnosis is generally avoided and the suggestion put in place that those receiving healing take diagnostic advice from GPs and other medical professionals.

Diakka - A word coined by A. J. Davis to describe naughty, mischievous or foolish spirits.

Dianetics - In scientology this is the technique and ability used to look at and be aware of past lives and experiences.

Dice Test - Some psychics claim the ability to predict or at least influence the way dice fall and have taken tests to prove their abilities.

Dicyanin Screens - Were devised by Dr Walter J. Kilner at St Thomas's Hospital. He hypothesised the view that following forced tiring of the eye or fatigue, that it could be made for a short period to see waves or vibrations outside the normal capability of sight more clearly. In more modern times goggles similar to motorcycle goggles, generally described as Kilner Goggles, or other rather less respectful titles, have been claimed to produce similar results.

Direct Drawing and Painting - Many psychic artists and mediums have produced drawings and paintings, the premise being that it is a spirit from the other world that controls the artist's hand. Famous practitioners include David Duguid, the Bangs Sisters and Coral Polge.

Direct Voice - The phenomena where a spirit from the other side speaks through a voice box created within the medium or through an artificial larynx, generally created by ectoplasmic type material drawn from within the medium. On occasions the voice can be a perfect replication of a spirit known to people present. This is a difficult form of mediumship as it requires a medium, and a guide and spirit from the other side who have experience in forming and manipulating the larynx or voice box. Sometimes the sound is very quiet and in the past a megaphone or trumpet which would sometimes float around the room independently would be used. Today professional amplification equipment such as microphones, PAs and similar equipment are available to assist. In mine, and many other mediums' opinion, this work can be performed in ordinary daylight or electrical lighting, whereas others insist on dim or other forms of night lighting or darkness.

Direct Voice Telephone - J. B. McIndoe invented the direct voice telephone, a simple microphone and transmitter attached to the medium's throat. Those present are then linked to the transmitter by a telephone-type receiver. Quite successful results were claimed under experimental conditions with the medium Andrew McCreadie.

Direct Writing - Writing that is produced with neither pen, pencil or other writing implements but simply through the movement of hands and fingers. Popular in the time of Eusaphia Paladino with claims made that some messages had been written inside sealed boxes. Although interesting to the Spiritualist this type of work has often been associated with magicians and fraudulent exponents of claimed psychical abilities.

Disassociation - A word used in psychic research to describe an independent act which seems to happen without obvious influence of any individual, medium or psychic's will.

Discarnate - Meaning not to be in possession of a physical body, often used descriptively of a spirit person, i.e. discarnate spirit.

Divination - To look for that which is hidden or more commonly, predict matters for someone else such as in astrology, palmistry and tarot cards. It should not really be considered as a normal part of a medium's work or considered within Spiritualism itself, but some mediums have made predictions or prophesies that have come true after being given such evidence by spirits.

Divining Rod - Traditionally a branch is cut from a hazel tree and a twig is made from it which dowsers hold, generally suspended or tensioned against fingers and thumbs. When water, or other wished for things are found, it is claimed the twig will either bend downwards, or in other directions, or that the person using the divining rod will feel a change in the muscles of the arms or other indicators, physical or mental.

Dixon, Jeane - Born 1918. One of America's most famous psychics who is claimed to have had some amazing predictions come true including the assassination of President John F. Kennedy and for many years was considered perhaps the leading light if not the very best psychic in the United States. Jeane Dixon came from Washington and was considered to have developed her abilities from a very early age.

Dixon Smith, Colonel - Wrote several theories based on Quantum Theory which he considered might be accountable for the penetration of the spirit world or existence of the higher life linkable with our physical world.

Djin - A word from ancient Arabia that in its simplest translation means 'elementals'. In some books the Djin are described as terrible evil spirits, perhaps even demons, yet some would claim the word Genie, as in 'Genie of the bottle', is also a derivation of Djin and a much kinder spirit.

Doctor - Many Spiritualists today and certainly some parapsychologists study for PhDs in parapsychology, though generally it is something that has to be studied as part of, some might say quite unfairly, a traditional psychology degree rather than just in its own field.

Dolan, Mia - Star of TV programme about haunted homes, Mia is a psychic and clairvoyant who has also written three books and teaches psychic awareness and development classes, and demonstrates at halls and theatres in the UK.

Doorkeeper - Every individual and medium has a special guide believed to be responsible for keeping them safe and protecting them whilst they are working mediumistically. Many famous mediums of today and yesteryear considered their doorkeeper almost like their closest friend on the other side, and these guides are often Chinese, African or Native American Indians. All people, who whilst on earth, would have already been progressing spiritually before moving to the other side and taking up a doorkeeper role.

Doppelganger - The word used to describe an individual's double in this world, sometimes seen by others. In Spiritualism it is also a word that describes the physical and etheric body which are perfect copies of each other. Indeed the word Doppelganger can be simply translated as meaning astral body.

Double - Also known as the etheric and physical body.

Double Blind - A test procedure when neither experimenter or test subject has prior knowledge of the special areas to be tested in any experiment.

Dowding, Air Chief Marshall - Former head of the technical department of the Air Ministry and Commander in Chief of Fighter Command during the Battle of Britain during 1940. A tireless promoter of Spiritualism and committed Spiritualist, fine lecturer and author of books on Spiritualism.

Dowsing - Diving for water and other objects by pendulum, twig, dowsing rods and any other method using a weight supported by a cord. In modern times it is used in many fields, not just for finding water, such as healing, finding missing people, and even oil and places on maps.

Dreams - Learning to interpret your dreams can be a wonderful experience. Certainly in analysing your dreams you will learn to have a better understanding of your inner, deepest feelings and perhaps even deepest secrets. No-one will ever be a better expert at interpreting your dreams than you. Spiritualist mediums have written books about dream analysis including Philip Solomon's book The Dreamers Psychic Dictionary.

Dream Allegory - In Freudian psychology, dreams are said to be exaggerated outplays or where the dreamer acts out deep-seated wants or desires. They provide a sort of safety valve which allows us do to what we wish in the dream state without facing the difficulties we would if we did such things whilst awake.

Dream Communication - Many people have dreams of their loved ones and others coming to them in the dream state to simply communicate or offer advice. Some mediums have claimed incredibly accurate communication with the other side whilst dreaming.

Dreams, Pre-Cognitive - Some people have dreams that would seem to be pre-cognitive in nature or come true later on, but Spiritualists generally think of this type of dream as perhaps suggesting alternative pathways that might be applicable.

Drop-in Communicator - A spirit entity that joins séances uninvited. Tended to happen more in the past or in circles that do not have an experienced medium teacher present.

Dualism - In simple explanation the opposing forces of good and evil, right and wrong.

Dual Personality - A term applied by some psychiatrists and psychologists as an alternative to what mediums claim to be spirit links. However, research within Spiritualism suggests the link between mediums and spirits that are working with them is very rarely ever in conflict and definitely under the control of the medium, who grants permission to receive information from the other side. Conversely, the dual personality the psychiatrist may diagnose tends to control an individual without permission, sometimes at will and is better defined as a mental illness than mediumship.

Duguid, David (1832-1907) - A Scottish medium of great acclaim, also a fine psychic artist who produced some remarkable results even in pitch black darkness. Also had a great interest in spirit photography and dictated the original words of Prince Hafed, claimed confidante and friend of Jesus Christ in his lifetime and associate of the Magi.

Duncan, Helen - Famous medium of Scotland. Many considered her a wonderful instrument for spirit, but other important members of the Spiritualist movement challenged and disclaimed her work, eventually having her taken to court and convicted, painting her as a witch more than a medium. To this day there are those who fight for and insist a pardon be appropriate for Helen Duncan. As the years have rolled by it has come to light that she perhaps did on occasion act fraudulently when under extreme pressure to deliver mediumistically, but there is overwhelming evidence from respected authorities to suggest she was a genuine gifted medium.

Dunne, J. W. - Brought into being the understanding of the philosophical concept of how time works, its relevance to the universe and the veridical position of dreams. He wrote extensively on serialism, presenting the opinion that men and women's consciousness follows a path set out through various events he called the 'travelling now', which he felt might be relevant to possible pre-visions by the widening of the perceptive field of abilities during the sleep state.

Dweller at the Threshold - Words more often used in occult language to describe an individual spirit or entity. Very similar to the doorkeeper guide in Spiritualism.

Dynamistograph - This was an instrument invented by the Dutch physicist Dr Matla and Dr Zaalberg van Zelst, apparently under spirit guidance. It was claimed the instrument worked. It could be placed in a room and through a window a dial could be viewed which would highlight letters that had intelligent meaning and proposed communication from the spirit world.

E

Earthbound - A term often used to describe Spirits who remain close to the earth plane linked by attachments they cannot give up or, more often than not, refuse to accept they are dead. Sometimes these spirits are misinterpreted as being ghosts.

Earthquake Effect - An experience alleged to have happened at some of D. D. Home's séances when the whole of the séance room shook as if in an earthquake.

Ecstasy - When an individual reaches a very exhilarated state. Some mediums seem to be like this just after coming out of trance mediumship or doing other work.

Ectoplasm - A liquid of translucent quality best described as white which generally comes from the mouth of a physical medium.

Eddy, Mary Baker - American founder of the Christian Science movement.

Edward, John - American medium given great acclaim for his ability to demonstrate mediumship, not only to audiences but on television too. Something of a forerunner in the field. Born and brought up on Long Island, New York, Edward showed his psychic abilities from a very young age but really only started to develop and become a famous psychic after meeting Lydia Clar, who made him more aware of his abilities and helped him to decide he would work full time as a professional medium. John Edward is now considered one of America's best psychic mediums and also the author of several best-selling books, but it is perhaps his TV programme nationally syndicated across the States, 'Crossing Over with John Edward', which has made him a psychic superstar.

Edwards, Glynn - Excellent present-day medium. Born in Liverpool, England, and also speaks with great authority on the philosophy of Spiritualism. A committed Spiritualist he is also interested in the teachings and wisdom of the East. He is held in respect within the movement as an original founder of the Gordon Higginson Fellowship and regular teacher at the Arthur Findlay College. Sometimes known as Devadasa, and was a protégé to some extent of Gordon Higginson.

Edwards, Harry (1893-1976) - Probably the most famous healer in the world. From the 1940s until his death in 1946 it is claimed he healed thousands of people and also demonstrated his gift at some very major venues including the Royal Albert Hall, London. He also used to practice absent healing which led him to bring into being the so-called 'healing minute' whereby those who could not see him physically would be sent healing at ten o'clock every night. Edwards founded the Harry Edwards' Spiritual Healing Sanctuary in 1946 and was also one of the original members of the National Federation of Spiritual Healers (NFSH). His work is continued today at his sanctuary by present members.

EEG - Electro-encephalography. Electronic method which records various levels of electrical responses from the human brain.

Ego - An individual's perception of his or herself, and abilities and potential.

Electrical Phenomena - Has been witnessed and seen on many occasions surrounding the physical body of mediums and other psychics as bright-light energy.

Electronic Communication - Many electronic experts for many years now have striven to build machines using electronic apparatus and means so that those without mediumistic ability would be able to tune in to the spirit world.

Electronic Voice Phenomena - Many people are now interested in recording the voices of discarnate bodies and also examining white noise, usually recorded digitally and then examined in close detail on an appropriate computer program.

Elemental - A term used to describe a nature spirit associated to the four elements of air, earth, water and fire, although in

Spiritualist circles you may also hear the term used to describe a discarnate entity, generally of low intellect or ability to communicate in a sensible and constructive manner.

Elemental Spirits - Spirits or entities considered relevant to the four elements of air, earth, fire and water.

Elementary - A term used in occult schools to describe some hauntings and even poltergeist-type phenomena. In some Spiritualist schools it may be used to describe the after-death overcoat of the physical body left behind only slowly disintegrating and giving up the spirit completely. This would not be accepted however in Spiritualistic doctrine.

Elongation - An unusual phenomenon that is said to have happened to some mediums, notably D. D. Home, with the claim that some mediums change in height or that arms and legs seem to become shorter or longer independently. Also alleged to have been experienced by Florence Cook, Palandino and others.

Emanations - Radiation of different forces are recognised and accepted in science. Some feel that those who have not yet been discovered may be relevant to matters of a psychical nature such as psychometry and dowsing. Even the production of ectoplasm may be appropriate to emanations as yet not understood scientifically.

Empathy - A basic requirement of all mediums and healers, means a wish to help others.

Engram - A word from scientology describing a hurtful mental image seen or felt from bad experiences in a past incarnation.

Enochian Language - This is the language claimed to be spoken and used by angels.

Entering the Silence - A short period of time is usually required by most mediums before they work in any way. At one time Spiritualist churches also observed a brief silence for attunement between the two worlds to commence, although this doesn't happen so much today.

Entity - A word to describe an individual discarnate spirit with a personality of its own.

Equinox - This is the time or point when the sun just starts to cross the celestial equator. This happens twice a year when night and day are of exactly the same length throughout the world and was the basis of our calendar measurements of time throughout the world.

Eschatology - Parts of theology and philosophy which address the end of physical matter and the future states of being.

Esoteric - Knowledge which can only be understood and appreciated by initiation, study and spiritual progression. Considered vital in the New Age movement and yet in Spiritualism the understanding of communication with the other world and the teaching of wise teachers and guides is considered a practical science, not really needing initiation or compliance.

ESP - Simply means extra-sensory perception.

Essenes - A very old Jewish sect who had high ideals and morals and were believed operational in the Middle East at the time of Jesus Christ. They may have origins that link to Buddhism, and the countries of Egypt and India (see Dead Sea Scrolls).

Estep, Sarah - Founded the American association of Electronic Voice Phenomena (EVP) and conducted much early research. Also a published author important for those researching EVP, especially in America.

Ether - That which is all around everything within the universe. Spiritualists consider the ether to be around us all the time, that the world is never silent and that if you listen even in the quietest places, you will still hear the buzz of the ether. It is also believed the ether permeates environment and links to both the earthly and spirit world.

Ethereal - Of heaven or heavenly

Etheric Body - The spirit of the physical body which goes on after death. Sometimes described as the double.

Etheric Plane - This is the spirit world on a level that is very close or adjacent to the Earth, that Spiritualists believe all of our loved ones and, indeed, all who pass to the other side go to before settling on a level appropriate to an individual's spiritual development or level of progression at time of death. This is the plane or level that is most communicative and where messages are given to our world.

Etheric Senses - You learn to have etheric senses through development. Those who become mediumistic or to a lesser degree, psychically capable, have to develop more finely tuned etheric senses.

Ethics - In the doctrine of Spiritualism the view may be put forward that the four main values or ethics are moral goodness, truth, altruism and understanding of retribution hereafter for all the good or bad you do in any life form.

ETP - Extra-Temporal Perception.

Euthanasia - Many people today take the view that under the right conditions a terminal illness or loss of quality of life, it may be appropriate for a doctor, relative or loved one to bring an early end to another's time in this world. Spiritualists do not accept this, believing that every second of our life in this world, pleasurable or painful, is part of our training or progression before moving onto the transition to the higher life, although a small minority of Spiritualists have expressed the view today that if the motives for termination of life are entirely humane it may not be considered an unspiritual act.

Evangelist - Originally seen as one of the authors of the four Christian gospels. In more modern times a member of the clergy, preacher of the gospels and follower of the religion of Evangelism would also be called by this title.

Evans, W. H. - British trance medium, also author of numerous books about Spiritualism and a person who spoke out publicly to promote Spiritualistic doctrine.

Everett Alkin, Lee - Respected British medium and psychic healer and author. Interesting books include The Happy Medium, Kind Of Loving and Celebrity Regressions. She brought into being the House of Spirit Healing and Development Centre and at one time was the long-term girlfriend of British pop singer Billy Fury, later married to famous British disc jockey, Kenny Everett.

Everitt, Mrs Thomas - British medium credited with good ability as a direct voice medium who in particular produced loud clear voices with little use of aids. Sir William Crookes, and other important people of her day were convinced of her abilities for which she also was claimed never to have charged or made a profit.

Evidence - This word is often used descriptively when a message is given from the other side and it is clearly accepted and recognised by the receiver.

Evil Eye - A long tradition or perhaps legend, is that some people have the ability to bring misfortune or unbalance people simply by looking at them, usually described as giving them the evil eye.

Evil Spirits - Since time immemorial men and women have referred to evil spirits. They are spoken of in all the great books of history. Sometimes all spirits have been described as evil when not understood by those who make such comments, mainly through ignorance or fear. However, there are spirits who are extremely bad as there are living beings in our world who are extremely bad and would not change in the early days of their move over into the spirit world at the time of their physical death. Spiritualism believes however in ultimate progression for all and that eventually even evil must become good. Most modern mediums would advise against the use of Ouija boards or planchettes. This is where sensitive operators may pick up spirits that would wish to misguide them, act stupidly or even scare people in this world.

Evolution - Put forward by science as a fact, the theory that the higher forms of life developed from much earlier underdeveloped simple forms. Spiritual evolution is the learning and spiritual understanding of our world and our continuous existence in higher levels of existence.

Evocation - To call up or summon any spirit, usually evil. Spiritualists never attempt to do this knowing that good spirits contact us if the need is there.

EVP - Electronic Voice Phenomena (see Electronic Voice Phenomena).

Exorcism - This is the ceremony within various religions where its clergy attempts to expel evil spirits and entities from individuals or places in our world. A quite common practice in the early traditional churches but not so operational today, often requiring permission of high-ranking clergy and for a specialist priest or minister to be brought in to conduct the exorcism. In the Spiritualist church the treatment for such situations can tend to be a fairly routine exercise usually conducted by a rescue medium on his or her own or with the support or help of a rescue circle. The difficult spirit or entity is offered the opportunity to talk to the medium or others present. It is encouraged to consider the advice that there is nothing for it in this world and it would be much better to join loved ones or those that can help find real happiness in the spirit world. Some mediums claim to have the ability to restrain and control the activities of such spirits too, others that the suggestion to pass over can only be made and jointly agreed with the spirit entity.

Exoteric - Opposite in meaning to esoteric. In simple terms, not secret.

Experiment - Many experiments or tests have been conducted on mediums and psychics to prove or disprove their gift.

Externalised Impression - During training mediums and psychics will be taught to appreciate and understand an externalised impression. This is something they believe has been received outside of their consciousness, but has really come from their imagination or own thoughts.

Extra - A word that describes any unexplained appearance of a figure generally on a photograph, that has occurred without any influence, interference from human hand or digital enhancement.

Extra-Sensory Perception (ESP) - Scientific term for perception of something without use of any of the recognised channels of sense. The most famous experiments to test ESP were probably organised by Professor J. B. Rhine of Duke University, North Carolina, USA, who looked at and produced evidence that statistically suggested there was evidence of telepathic ability present in some men and women that could not really be gauged by any known scientific or physical law at the time of his tests. In Spiritualism however, the medium's role is to prove by evidence the existence of the afterlife and life here ever after, not to produce results through telepathy.

Extra Temporal Perception (ETP) - In simple explanation, ESP as looked at through distance and space as well as time.

Extra-Terrestrial - An entity or being generally from outer space or from another planet would be described as ET - extra-terrestrial.

Extrovert - Describes an individual whose character is extremely outgoing; the opposite of introvert. In Spiritualism neither type of personality is considered either better or worse for development, though some schools of training might suggest extroverts make the better mediums and introverts the better healers. In my experience this is not so.

Eyeless Sight - An ability claimed by some mediums to see with the eyes completely closed and to actually view from the skin or outer levels of the etheric body around the physical being. Some tests have been claimed where mediums have described what is behind them or in other rooms. Tests for eyeless sight have become less popular today.

F

Facsimile Writing - Some very spectacular reproductions of hand-written, typed or computer word-processed text including the words of some very famous people, have been written by automatists. In the past interesting cases were those of the work of Oscar Wilde, produced through Esther Dowden and others.

Fairies - Evidence for the existence of little people in Ireland has long since been believed. Likewise these little people have been claimed to be existent in England too (see Sir Arthur Conan Doyle).

Faith - Simply means to have belief in what one cannot have proved or cannot see or touch. Of course, in Spiritualism you will not be expected to have faith, for it is the basis of the religion to give proof at many of its church services and other meetings, of its positive existence.

Faith Healing - This is healing which is said to be brought about by the person receiving it having faith in its success, usually from some divine power they truly believe in. This is different to spiritual healing where even the receiver who has no faith or belief still receives healing and can be made better and balanced. Places such as Lourdes in France have long been visited by those who believe in faith healing.

Fakirs - These are important members of eastern religious movements who are said to have highly gifted psychic powers and abilities. Some Fakirs practice self-mortification and inflict wounds and injuries upon themselves. There are even claims that some have the ability to be buried alive and to put themselves into a self-induced or cataleptic state that slows the heartbeat and breathing almost to a stop and allows survival when later recovered from such graves.

False Awakening - Where an individual believes they are awake but are actually in the dream state.

Familiar - A word which has its origins in mediaeval times particularly in witchcraft crimes where those being judged would be claimed to have a familiar such as a cat or goat. Many wise men and women and indeed natural mediums were probably hung on such flimsy claims, although few were actually burned at the stake as many believe.

Famous Returns - From time immemorial there have been claims of the famous returning to present themselves or prove their continuing existence through mediums in this world. Professor Hans Holzer, considered by many as the leading investigator of the paranormal in modern times, conducted séances for people such as Elvis Presley's family and genuine members of royalty. Famous family members on the other side came through and gave messages that positively proved truthful because they could only be confirmed by members of the celebrity or person's close family. Presidents, kings, queens and others have all been seen in quite physical forms throughout history.

Faraday Cage - A metal cage that operates in such a way that it cannot be penetrated by radio frequencies or waves.

Fatalism - The belief that everything that happens to you is determined by a divine higher power and cannot be changed.

Feedback - All good mediums and psychics should accept feedback, compliments or constructive criticism to develop their abilities.

Feng Shui - An ancient Chinese art that investigates energies that are hidden from most people. People who really understand the discipline of Feng Shui have a great knowledge of Kung-Lei, translation dragon paths, which might best be described as similar to meridian or ley lines. Feng Shui practitioners can advise you on the best way to set out your home, furniture, etc. The art was first written by Yang Yun-Sung. Read further for a better understanding of the subject.

Findhorn - A spiritual community that came into being in 1962 in Scotland. Gardens were laid out that yielded plants and flowers in fantastic large sizes and with great growth. The organisers claimed they received advice for their planting and management from the spirit world and spirits of the natural world. Peter Caddy and Dorothy Maclean planted the first site. It is now recognised as one of the model communities linked to the New Age movement of the sixties and seventies. Findhorn has flourished and demonstrated its ability to function as a successful community home and democratic business and of course produce wonderful garden/farm produce all from within its own community. Many Spiritualists support and have visited Findhorn.

Findley, J. Arthur, OBE, JP (1883-1964) - Not a medium himself but made an extensive study of all aspects of Spiritualism, wrote many books including, Trilogy, and a most important book to Spiritualists, The Rock of Truth. In 1964 he gave one of his country homes, Stansted Hall in Essex, as a complete donation to the Spiritualist National Union (SNU) with the instruction it was to be developed into a college for all to have the opportunity to study Spiritualism and psychic science. The SNU most gladly brought to fruition Arthur Findlay's instructions and called the hall The Arthur Findlay College in his name. Today it offers training to students from all over the UK and indeed the world. Findlay also came to the rescue of Psychic News when it was in some difficulties in its early days with financial help. It is today the world's most respected and established newspaper of its kind.

Finite - Complete end or termination, finished.

Fire, Immunity from - Many psychics and Fakirs have presented immunity to fire.

Fire Walking - An ancient practice from the East practised today by many, including those on management or bonding training courses, etc.

First Course - Synonymous with a deity or origin of the world, or the start of all things to come.

Flint, Leslie - Truly one of the great names of Spiritualism. The accuracy of messages given from the other side to some very famous people in this world meant Flint was always in great demand. In his autobiography Voices in the Dark, there are descriptions of how some of those testing him would insist that he was heavily bound, gagged and locked in various boxes but still Spirit would come through with physical evidence and clear voice to prove the truth of life hereafter. He worked in many countries all over the world demonstrating his abilities and was just as comfortable in a small room or large theatre. A very important person to modern Spiritualism. Some of his work is well-recorded on audio tape and now being transferred to digital formats for future research.

Flower Clairsentience - This is generally a demonstration of mediumship whereby those in attendance bring along a flower that is placed on the rostrum of the medium. By holding it and looking at it a reading is given to the various individuals. Though considered by some to be truly part of mediumship, by others it is considered to have only psychic associations.

Flying Saucers - In modern times there would seem to be overwhelming evidence to suggest that flying saucers of some sort exist. It still remains to be proven whether they are of normal or unexplainable origins. Spiritualists are very much divided upon their truth and within the doctrine of the religion there seems to be no definite view suggested either way as to whether they exist or not.

Focal Person - Individuals who are under poltergeist-type attacks may be described as the focal person in such an incident.

Fodor, Dr Nandor - Psychoanalyst of Hungarian birth and great metaphysical knowledge, a lecturer and author of numerous books important in psychical research including the excellent Encyclopaedia of Psychic Science.

Ford, Arthur - Spiritualist medium from the USA, an original founder member of the International General Assembly of Spiritualists (IGAS). The medium became aware of his abilities during the First World War, when he was given the names of comrades who were later reported on the 'Killed in Action' lists shortly afterwards. After the war he studied psychic phenomena in great depth and demonstrated not only in America but Great Britain too, where Sir Arthur Conan Doyle allegedly described the demonstration he witnessed as one of the finest he had seen and most evidential to those receiving evidence from the other side.

Fortean Phenomena - Named after American psychic

researcher and author Charles Fort. Fortean phenomena are anything outside of the physical norm but generally extremely bizarre or considered incredibly paranormal.

Fortune Telling - A form of prediction generally seen at psychic fairs, practised by some gipsies and some psychics. Not part of Spiritualism or a medium's work.

Fortune-Telling Act - Closely linked to the Vagrancy Act, it was taken out of English Law after the introduction of the Fraudulent Mediums Act 1951. Before that, mediums could be considered for prosecution fines and possibly even jail time by simply being labelled alongside fortune-tellers. Luckily, today they have proper legal status, are part of a recognised accepted religion and able to display their gifts and ability for themselves, and of course most important, other men and women of this world who need to know that life never ends.

Four Noble Truths - See Buddhism.

Fourth Dimension - Many Spiritualists believe in several levels of existence in the higher world with the suggestion there are seven levels that progress towards the godhead, the fourth level or dimension being one of them.

Fox, George (1624-1691) - Founded the Quaker's Movement or Society of Friends. Their doctrine suggests that at around 19 years of age Fox was given a divine message or command to leave behind all family, all links from his life and to speak out against formalism in all religions.

Fox Sisters - Kate-Margaret and Leah authored a book, The Missing Link, claiming the answer to this historic question. They are of course acclaimed by many as being the original founders of Spiritualism in 1848 after conducting communication with spirits in the other world through raps and taps on tables in Hydesville, USA, where they lived. They also claimed to have formulated a code whereby messages could also be passed between them and the higher life, what many considered at that time as simply dead people. In many ways it is wrong to consider the Fox Sisters the starting point of Spiritualism. Many people believe the ancient druids and certainly in much more modern times the Native American Indian people practised communication with the spirit world in far more advanced ways than simple raps or taps. Nevertheless the Fox Sisters are important in the history of modern Spiritualism.

Fraud - People who deliberately fake any paranormal phenomena or con the general public through means of sleight of hand. In the case of a medium, he or she who pretends to have communication from Spirit but actually intentionally makes up messages.

Fraudulent Mediums Act - Was placed in English Statute Law in 1951 after great championing efforts by Tom Brookes, the MP for Normanton, West Riding in England. Importantly, in English Law it replaced the Vagrancy Act, which was repealed. Before that, any medium genuine or fraudulent risked prosecution or imprisonment on most inappropriate or flimsy grounds.

Freemasons - The Freemasons have been described as a secret, close-kept organisation which may have originally evolved from mediaeval stonemasons. Many believe the order now includes business professionals and people from all social standing who help each other. Membership is only open to men and has included people believed to have been both incredibly famous and interested in Spiritualism such as Winston Churchill and George Washington.

Free Thinkers - People who are not dogmatic about anything and believe it is important to rationalise everything in this world, rarely bound by the doctrine of one particular belief or one religion. Spiritualism has had its truth examined by those looking at it as free thinkers. Spiritualism never demands belief and makes welcome those from all religions and faiths, even agnostics and atheists, with the hope that free thinking will allow them to find what they believe is the truth of Spiritualism and life ever after.

Friends, Society of Quakers - Non-formalist religion and society founded around 1666 by George Fox of Leicester, East Midlands, England. The name of Quakers and sometimes Shakers, particularly in America, was a derisive term made by others outside their society whose attention was drawn to the unusual trembling action of the friends as they were inspired to speak or address others. On occasions this type of trembling action affects very good mediums in the Spiritualist movement when either speaking from the rostrum or when moving into the early stages of trance mediumship.

Fry, Colin - British Spiritualist medium based in Brighton. A medium for many years, much of his early work was as a physical medium operating under the pseudonym of 'Lincoln'. He continues to demonstrate mediumship, influenced by one of his guides, Magnus. Colin was very much involved with the Noah's Ark Society which promoted physical mediumship and regularly held séances for its members and other guests. Colin shot to success as one of Britain's best known mediums on his successful TV programme known as the 'Sixth Sense'. A close friend of Tony Stockwell, the two men sometimes demonstrate at theatres together and Colin regularly appears on his own at such events too. He is also the author of several books. He also started up a psychic college in Sweden which unfortunately has now closed. A good worker for Spirit.

G

Ganzfeld - A test for ESP which often requires the person being tested to wear special goggles over the eyes and headphones whilst common radio noise such as 'white noise' can also be heard in the headphones.

Garrett, Eileen J. (1893-1970) - Considered by the world's leading authority on the paranormal, Professor Hans Holzer, as one of the greatest mediums of her time. Born in Ireland, Eileen was much travelled but conducted most of her measured and tested work in the United States. Very much a modern medium for her time she is certainly worthy of further study by those interested in mediumship generally. Her daughter, Eileen Coly, is the president of the parapsychology foundation in the US and her granddaughter Lisett Coly is the present director of this highly respected American organisation. Harry Price was most impressed with Garrett and followed her career with close interest although they never actually worked together.

Gascoyne, Duncan P. - MSNU. President of the Council and chairman of the Arthur Findlay College. A man who has done much good work for the Spiritualist movement generally.

Geley, Dr Gustav (1868-1924) - Highly respected French psychical researcher and director of the Institut Metapsychique Internationale. Claims were made of unexplainable manifestations and other psychic phenomena produced in his laboratory under the strictest test conditions, and he wrote many books on psychic research, including the important From the Unconscious to the Conscious.

Geller, Uri - Born 1946. An Israeli psychic who has received great acclaim for his apparent abilities to bend metal objects by simply touching, stroking or looking at them. At the peak of his career in the 1970s Uri demonstrated his paranormal activities to television audiences worldwide and is still of great interest to the general public even today.

Geomancy - Method of divination that looks at figures and lines.

Gestic Magic - Magic considered to come from the dark side, through invoking evil spirits and making use of their assistance.

Ghost - The appearance or unexplained vision of an individual who is definitely dead. There have been visions of people who are still alive too.

Ghost Club - Originally came into being in 1862 to investigate psychic phenomena generally and had some most distinguished original members. In 1881 Sir William Barrett, FRS, instigated a lot more investigation and encouraged further members to join. Harry Price, famed ghost hunter of the 30s and 40s, was another important member, as is Peter Underwood, a writer of many modern ghost books today.

Ghoul - Describes a spirit said to be of a lower order. In its Arabian origins claimed to have hung around places of burial looking to draw or feed on the energy of the dead.

Glastonbury Scripts - A collection of automatic communications received from the spirit world between 1918 and 1927, culminating in the publication of nine booklets. Many mediums were involved in this, including Hester Dowden and Margery Crandon, in efforts to locate unearthed parts of Glastonbury Abbey and the profile of its perceived history through their mediumship.

Glossolalia - Speaking in other tongues.

Glottologues - Mediums who can speak in unrecognisable or unknown tongues and language.

Gnani Yoga - The pathway to attainment of complete wisdom.

Gnomes - Nature Spirits that are said to be closely linked with the earth. There are several different names of these spirits. They are often claimed when viewable to clairvoyants to be seen as small humans perhaps with dwarf characteristics.

Gnostics - Members of a very early Christian sect who claimed special wisdom of both the spiritual and esoteric nature. Believed to have propagated a very early suggestion of the divinity of Jesus.

God - The supreme being. Spiritualists sometimes refer to God as Mother/Father God, the Great White Spirit, the Supreme Spirit, the Great Spirit, and of course by the original term God. Terms may differ between Spiritualists who follow the SNU doctrine and Christian Spiritualists.

Gow, David - Editor in chief of Light, journalist and writer who gave up a traditional career to dedicate his life to committing in print his belief that Spiritualism would become the future religion of the world.

GWCSA - Greater World Christian Spiritualists Association (see Christian Spiritualists).

Grant, Russell - Probably the best-known astrologer in the United Kingdom, recognised worldwide. Very much a man of the media with an outstanding personality that works well on TV. Perhaps less well-known, Russell Grant is also a fine and evidentially accurate medium who follows the religion of Spiritualism.

Greater World, The - Founded in Britain by 1931 as part of the Christian Spiritualist division, the original president being Alfred Morris. They now have worldwide recognition and the teachings of their pathway are built upon the words of Zodiac, the guide of Miss Winifred Moyes, a much acclaimed voice trance medium and the original editor of Greater World. Zodiac is claimed by some Christian Spiritualists to have commentaries included in the Bible (Mark 12:28-35) (see Christian Spiritualists). They can be contacted at GWCSA, 3-5 Conway Street, London, W1P 5HA.

Green - The colour green is often active in the human aura and is considered by some who see it to represent intelligence and healing.

Green Man - An ancient symbol claimed to be of Celtic origin. Many Spiritualists today are interested in early belief structures, mysticism, etc., and the Green Man is a very important character.

Grey - When seen as a colour in the human aura it is not considered to be of a good nature and the Spiritualist medium healer who has the ability to see such colours may be drawn to give healing in that area.

Group Soul - A most interesting description of soul relationships whereby several souls are joined together in group evolution. Involves the idea that animals and pets, which some Spiritualists believe do not have a singular soul (many others disagree with this), progress to the higher world collectively.

Guardian Angel - Many Spiritualists believe that a specific spirit or more appropriately angel of the higher realms takes on the job of protector and helper of every individual right from birth. Some Spiritualists consider this to be the guide they refer to as the Doorkeeper.

Guest de Swarte, Lyn - Former editor of Psychic News. Continues to write columns for various magazines and media outlets and is a good demonstrating Spiritualist medium. Lyn also wrote a very useful book seen as one of the best introductions to an understanding of the religion of Spiritualism entitled Principles of Spiritualism. It would be of great use to those new to this way of life or looking for a very easy to read introduction.

Guide - This is the word Spiritualists use to describe the control who acts in a protective and working role between the medium and any other discarnate spirits who might wish to communicate with people in our world.

Gurdjieff, George Ivanovich (1872-1949) - Born in Russia, an acclaimed Spiritual leader and founder member of a movement based and built upon the doctrines of wisdom and enlightenment through heightened self-awareness, mediation techniques. He had many followers in America and Europe and is considered by many as one of the greatest mystical, spiritual teachers of his time, yet by others as a charlatan.

Gurney, Edmond (1847-1888) - A highly respected British investigator of psychic matters and first honorary secretary of the SPR. Wrote the highly acknowledged Phantasms of the Living in co-authorship with Podmore and Myers and is claimed to have communicated on a regular basis with Sir Oliver Lodge through the mediumship of several channels.

Guru - The Hindu term for teacher or wise one.

H

Hades - Known as the place of fire and brimstone to some people. Perhaps in some ways descriptive of purgatory in the Catholic religion. May also be the first level of existence where bad or evil people from this world go to, but with the opportunity for them to progress and leave it behind eventually. Some Spiritualists believe there is no such place as Hades or Hell at all.

Hafan-y-Coed - Spiritual development centre situated in the Brecon Beacons National Park of which the author is a certified tutor. Many courses are offered in Spiritualist and psychic development, and others of an esoteric nature, by well-known mediums and teachers.

Hafed, The Prince of Persia - Is claimed to have communicated to this world through the mediumship of David Duguid at the house of H. Nisbet, the famous Glasgow publisher. In well over 40 sittings Nisbet told the wonderful story of this warrior prince who not only fought against an invading Arabian army but was so wonderfully gifted and wise that he was accepted into the order of the Magi, reaching the high position of Arch Magus, describing ancient lives of very important people of Persia, Greece Egypt, Babylon and Judea. Perhaps the most interesting of his communications was when he advised and arranged the travels of the three wise men to the birthplace of Jesus Christ, advised by his guardian spirit to undertake this journey with two other Magi and to take special gifts to the birthplace of the baby Jesus. Much information was communicated about the so called lost years of Jesus' early life. He is also claimed to have met St Paul in Athens. Obviously this was a wonderful story that fascinated many and was published along with some excellent illustrations in 1876.

Halo - The outline of light often exemplified in paintings and drawings of early important Christians such as Jesus, Mary and the saints. Some Spiritualists feel there may be a link with the aura that is seen by clairvoyants and other sensitives around the heads of special people today.

Hallowe'en - All Hallows Eve falls on the 31st October, the preceding day before All Saints' Day, and is a time when spirits are claimed to be able to draw close to the earth plane with the veil between the two worlds at its thinnest. It may have some possibility of truth inherent but its modern trick or treat aspects, particularly in America, mean it is not considered of great importance to most Spiritualists.

Halls of Learning - Some Spiritualists believe there are places in the higher life where records are kept giving knowledge of everything that has ever happened or will ever happen in the universe. Some individuals have claimed to visit the halls of learning through meditation or during their dream state.

Hallucination - Perceiving something to have a basis in truth where no objective proof is available, therefore some claim not scientifically acceptable or to be believed in.

Hamilton-Parker, Craig and Jane - Fine practising mediums based in Hampshire, England, who regularly appear on TV and radio, and have produced an incredible website, www.psychics.co.uk, that covers a multitude of subjects to do with the psychic world. They also train and develop other psychics and mediums and have appeared on television documentaries and acted as consultants to TV programme makers.

Hari Krishna - A faith probably started around 1948 by the Indian guru A. C. Bhaktivedanta Swami Prabhupada. It became incredibly popular in the Western world in the mid-60s and shaven-headed devotees in saffron robes would often be seen clinking cymbals as they chanted 'Ha-re Krish-na' repeatedly. The complete mantra is as follows: 'Hare Krishna/hare Krishna/Krishna Krishna/hare hare/hare rama/ hare rama/rama rama/hare hare'. Many Spiritualists in the 60s, 70s and 80s took an interest in and investigated the Hari Krishna Movement.

Hatha Yoga - A spiritual pathway, and also physical lifestyle and culture that leads to discipline and satisfaction.

Hatton, Eric L. - MSNU. President of the Spiritualists' National Union between 1993 and 1996, he retains an honorary presidential role today and runs the highly respected Stourbridge Spiritualist Church in the West Midlands.

Haunting - Unexplainable disturbances or appearances attributed to someone or something not of the living world. Manifestations can include noises, and appearances of spectres of varying degrees of opacity. Some parapsychologists and many Spiritualists believe hauntings happen on a regular reported basis after an unfortunate incident in this life, such as someone being killed, imprints a replay into the ether that can be seen by sensitive people. There are claims that pleasant situations such as a lover's kiss may also trigger such events too.

Healer - Anyone who has the ability to heal others and proves this to be factual should be considered a healer.

Healing Circle - Healing circles are generally designed and put together to give those interested in healing the opportunity to understand and develop this very special form of mediumship. Today, some circles also allow certain students to learn about other methods of healing such as Reiki, crystal healing, etc., but most will still basically teach spiritual healing (see Spiritual Healing).

Healing, Faith - Some religions believe it is a basic requirement to have faith in the person delivering healing, or your god, if healing is to take place and be effective. Not a view generally taken by many Spiritualists who believe healing works whenever it is given or sent whether believed in or not.

Healing, Magnetic - Words first coined by Franz Mesmer, whereby mesmerism developed into hypnotherapy. Hypnotism might be used by a physician to cure patients.

Healing, Spirit - Many healers claim this is a spirit that works through them from the other side to heal individuals in this world. Very often this will be a doctor, surgeon or similar man or woman of medicine. Some such as Ray Browne claim to be the instrument of healing for Biblical icons such as St Paul. Some are influenced by medicine men of the Native American Indian tribes and others.

Hearn, Ronald L. - Respected British medium and author, a particularly interesting book of his is The Little Dutch Boy: Study in Psychic Communication.

Heaven - The place Christians believe to be there ultimately for all believers. Spiritualists believe progression must be made through several levels of higher existence before such a place can be reached and many teachers, past and present, have also hypothesised the view that the kingdom of heaven lies within the individual.

Hedonism - When thought of philosophically, some thinkers suggest that pleasure alone is the ultimate aim in men and women.

Heindel, Max - A writer of many books linked to the Rosicrucian way of life and also the signs of astrology. He also organised a healing sanctuary that operated for over 30 years with its practices grounded in astrological diagnosis followed by psychic treatments.

Hell - The suggested region of a place of eternal punishment for the evil in our world following death. Many Spiritualists believe like attracts like and that hell may be a place that such people gather together such as the first level of existence in the spirit world. Some Spiritualists believe there is no hell as such (see Hades).

Helper, Spirit - A word that simply describes a spirit from the other side, not necessarily cleverer than the person it works with in this world, though it is generally the case that they wish to help and guide an individual in our world on a specific spiritual or physical pathway. Generally that spirit has experience of and wisdom it can give to someone in this world.

Hermes - The Greek god of travellers and heavenly messengers, believed by many ancient civilisations to be the revealer of divine knowledge and wisdom.

Hermetic Order of the Golden Dawn (HOGD) - Originally founded in 1888 in London. Was a secret organisation and society that included many famous members including Constance Wilde, spouse of Oscar Wilde, the Irish poet William Butler Yates, and perhaps the most infamous of them all, Aleister Crowley, termed by the media of his day as the most evil man in the world. The founder of the order was believed to be S. L. MacGregor Mathers, who claimed that he received the wisdom and esoteric knowledge required to bring the order together from ascended masters and leaders whilst in a mediumistic trance-like state. The order closed its membership and came to an end in 1900.

Hex - To put a spell upon someone or curse them in an evil way is to 'hex' them.

Higginson, Mons Gordon - Born on 17th November, 1919, and claimed to be part of his mother's development circle by the age of three. Started to demonstrate mediumship in his early teens and quickly became one of the best mediums in the world. He sold out demonstrations at venues like London's Royal Albert Hall. In 1970 he became president of the Spiritualists National Union, serving in that role for more than 20 years. He also became principle of the Arthur Findlay College and is held in the highest esteem by almost everyone in the movement for having a wide ability in all mediumistic gifts, plus being credited as a fine teacher and inspiration for many of the young mediums who are practising today. He also had an open mind and interest in mystical subjects and other religions. Considered by many to be one of, if not the best, medium of his time. He passed to Spirit on the 18th January, 1983.

Higher Self - A description of the concept, looked for or searched for in the individual, through practices such as meditation, trance states, etc.

Hinduism - The largest religion practised by the people of India. Also practised by many Asian people in England and America today.

Hit - Information that is given from the other world to someone in this world which is extremely accurate would be considered a 'hit'. Sometimes under test conditions success from a medium or other sensitive is also called a hit.

Holloway, Gilbert - Dr Holloway was a Spiritualist medium who brought into being the so-called Christ Light Community organisation in Deming, New Mexico, where he proclaimed his ideas and views on metaphysics and gained a following.

Holy Grail, The - The search for a vessel of many individuals and groups said to have been used by Jesus Christ at the Last Supper or by some to have been the cup that caught the falling blood of the crucified Christ on the cross. Many legends suggest it may have been secreted at places such as Glastonbury, Scotland, near the Rosslyn Chapel and numerous other sites throughout the world. Many Spiritualists today believe the Holy Grail is symbolic of searching for knowledge and progression as an individual person.

Home Circle - One of the most important parts of the early Spiritualist movement were the home circles, dedicated places where dedicated spiritualists would meet, generally on a weekly basis, to link with the spirit world and progress mediumistically, individually and as a group. They would also discuss the philosophy and progress of Spiritualism for them and others as a way of life.

Home, Daniel Dunglas (1833-1886) - One of the most famous British Scottish mediums of all time, some claim perhaps the greatest medium of modern history. Eminent scientists and investigators of psychic phenomena all supported him as being incredibly gifted. Sir William Crookes and many others attested to levitation, an ability to touch fire without injury, produce music from instruments not present and just about every example of mediumship and psychical phenomena that any medium before or since has been able to present. A must-read-about person for anyone interested in demonstrational mediumship of his kind.

Horoscope - The map of the heavens and charts that astrologers draw up for individuals to advise of life possibilities. Astrology is not really a strong part of Spiritualism, but some Spiritualists use terms that have come from astrological doctrine and some astrologers are also Spiritualists and mediums.

Hot Reading - Where an incredibly accurate reading is given to someone but the medium has actually researched or been given prior information about the person they read for. Obviously fraudulent.

Houdini, Harry - Possibly the world's greatest magician and escapologist. Had a special friendship with Sir Arthur Conan Doyle. The two men fell out when Houdini claimed that most mediumship was conjuring or 'sleight of hand' tricks. It is claimed that Sir Arthur's wife gave a mediumistic reading for Houdini purporting to come from his mother. Houdini was not happy that it was not given in Hebrew and with other events and facts that he felt were unsatisfactory. This was the final straw that ended their friendship permanently, though many people quite wrongly claim Houdini said all mediums were fraudulent. He did not, and throughout his life continued to search for the medium he felt could give him satisfactory proof of the afterlife.

Hudson, Dorothy - MSNU. One time president of the Spiritualists' National Union and a fine worker for Spiritualism.

Hugo, Victor (1802-1885) - A famous novelist who believed in Spiritualism and helped to bring some authority to the religion both in Britain and France.

Human Personality - In psychology personality is seen as the description of emotions, thoughts and behaviour patterns expressed in human beings (see Personality).

Huna - a spiritual religion from Hawaii that has elements of mediumship and healing inherent in it.

Hydesville - Many people claim Hydesville in America to be the birthplace of modern Spiritualism. It is a small area, part of the greater New York State and was the home of the Fox Sisters whose story of communication with spirits in 1848 is well told all over the world.

Hymns - The singing of hymns and praise is made use of in services in most Spiritualist churches and of course all other church services. In many cases the words of traditional hymns have been changed to make them more appropriate to Spiritualism. New ones have been written by Spiritualists and they all remain popular, although some Spiritualists today express the view that they have no place in the religion and should not be sung at all.

Hyperaesthesia - Incredibly heightened sensory perception and awareness.

Hyperamnesia - Simply means to work on improving memory power and to obtain faster sensitivity to other worldliness. More important in the fields of hypnotism really than Spiritualism but practised by some.

Hypnopompic Image - Images that are generally seen just at the time people wake up. Many people experience this; it may not necessarily be a spirit or paranormal experience.

Hypnosis - The level of suggestibility known as being in a state of hypnosis, developed from Franz Mesmer's early work in mesmerism.

Hypnotic Regression - Through hypnotherapy some Spiritualists think you can be taken back to view or gain knowledge from your past lives. They believe that reincarnation is a fact. Some Spiritualists accept this as being the truth, some claim emphatically that it is not.

Hypnotism - More often recognised today for its entertainment value, not really part of Spiritualism, though the practice of hypnotherapy may be used for regression to past lives, etc. Hypnotism is really the modern word for mesmerism.

Hyslop, James H. (1854-1920) - Important psychical researcher, studied at the University of Leipzig and Hopkins University obtaining a PhD in 1877. One of the first American professors to link psychology with psychic phenomena. In later life publicly announced he had communicated with family members in the spirit world and wrote extensively, including fine books such as Contact With The Other World, in 1919.

I

I Ching - The basis of Chinese philosophy. Relates to the dual cosmic consideration of yin and yang, which are both the physical and psychic principles of opposites, black and white, good and bad, etc.

Icke, David - Born 1952. A former professional goalkeeper for several British football clubs Icke became a television presenter and eventually spokesman for the Green Party. David suggests that he has developed a position of moral and political overviewer of world issues that bring New Age ideas, Spiritualism and many other doctrines into close comparison. He has also hypothesised the view that the world may be governed by various secret groups he collectively calls the Global Elite or Illuminati. In his early books David writes of several well-known mediums including Judith Hall, Philip Solomon and Betty Shine. David Icke is in many ways a brave man prepared to speak openly about what he believes to be the truth and important to others.

Identity, Proof of - Before any evidence from the other side is accepted as true spirit communication, it must prove beyond doubt that the spirit is recognised by someone in this world.

Ideoplasm - Another word for ectoplasm but that which can be formed into recognisable shapes for recognition by others.

Ignis Fatuus - These are the unusual lights that are seen in areas of marshland, swamps, mined land and unusually enough in cemeteries and graveyards. Generally thought of as natural gases that rise from the earth, some sensitives claim to have seen similar lights around unusual or sudden-death cases.

Illuminati - A word to describe a group of individuals who were members of secret societies, sects and groups that believe in 'illuminism', which in simple terms is the searching for spiritual and esoteric wisdom through the revelation from a higher spirit source alongside the search for human knowledge. The best-known order was operational in Bavaria in 1776 but reached out to many other parts of Europe and the world. The order of Illuminati is said to have included important people such as Franz Mesmer and the German writer and wordsmith Goethe.

Illuminism - See Illuminati.

Illusion - Something that is not real but is falsely recognised or interpreted as being real. Magicians perform illusions; they are not something that should be part of a genuine medium or psychic's demonstrations.

Imagery - When someone senses and creates images in their mind which may be visual but also have some audio context.

Immortality - Some Spiritualists believe in immortality, i.e. never dying, but in its proper context it should be applied as meaning no death and the truth of life here ever after and forever progressive.

Impersonation - Pretending to be someone else or imitating the voice of another's spirit. Their personality or character is claimed to manifest on some occasions .This may happen to inexperienced mediums where they are not properly protected or do not have a supportive guide in place to make sure such impersonation never happens.

Impression - Whereby some entities influence the mind of sensitive people, perhaps teaching them to play a musical instrument, speak with authority on an academic subject not known or studied by an individual.

Imprints - Spiritualists sometimes speak of imprints in the ether, a replay generally of an event in history that has been absorbed and recorded and can be sensed and played back by those of sensitive nature to such things.

Incubi/Succubae - Evil immoral spirits that were claimed to visit human beings whilst in the sleep state with the aim that they would succumb to their sexual advances. Some legends suggest such spirits were always attracted to the most pure, other legends that they found those of loose morals the most interesting with the view being that like attracts like. Other legends suggested they could take on the shape of kindly, handsome or beautiful individuals, only showing their true nature and likeness when they had finished the business they had come to the earth plane to practise. Considered unlikely and without any real substance of truth by Spiritualists.

Independent Voice - Words that describe psychical voice projected phenomena that do not need amplifying in any way, such as by a trumpet, megaphone, or in more modern times a microphone and amplifier.

Indirect Voice - When the voice from Spirit seems to be coming from somewhere else rather than the medium, it is described in spiritualistic terms as indirect voice communication.

Ineffable Name - Historically, this means the name of God but which must not be spoken.

Inexplicable - Word to describe out of the ordinary or unexplainable in physical or scientific terms.

Infinite - No end or no limit to possibilities, such as the Infinite God or Great White Spirit spoken of by Spiritualists.

Influence - Mediums and others often refer to a spirit influence. This tends to mean they are sensing or clairsentiently picking up energies that suggest communicable information for them or others.

Influenced Writing - To write with character and ability influenced by the thoughts of other people or entities.

Initiate - A person accepted into certain groups where mysteries, wisdom and other knowledge is made known to them.

Inspiration - Mediums will often describe being under the inspiration of Spirit, perhaps to speak with great knowledge on the philosophy of Spiritualism or other worldly knowledge or perhaps inspired to paint a particular portrait or landscape.

Inspirational Speaking - To address others without prompts or resorting to notes, usually with most important knowledge and wisdom for others. Inspirational speaking is sometimes given in different states of trance mediumship.

Inspirational Writing - More often called automatic writing, where the hand is under no physical control yet writes messages, draws symbols, or perhaps sketches. The writing is sometimes written at extremely high speed, well out of the normal capability of normal scribes.

Instinct - When someone is prompted to speak or take action that is important for them or others it is often based on the feelings known as instinct rather than logical reasoning.

Inspired Address - Mediums who serve Spiritualist churches and other meetings are generally expected today to give good evidence of survival after death but also as a general matter of requirement to be able to give an inspired address. This generally consists of a short speech which can be read from notes, of a philosophical or inspirational nature linked closely in content to Spiritualism as a way of life or religion.

Instrument - Some mediums prefer to be called instruments for Spirit rather than mediums.

Intellect - The area of the mind which understands and reasons accurately.

Intelligence - The capacity of the mind to reason out and make decisions.

Introvert - Describes a quiet person who tends to keep their own company and avoid making decisions or taking the lead in actions.

Intuition - Not really supernormal but rather the inner feelings that many have with regard to people and things that prove later to be accurate.

Invocation - A prayer that is usually spoken right at the start of a religious practice. A common occurrence at most Spiritualist churches before any service. Sometimes it is used to describe welcoming benevolent spirit beings to work with a medium.

Islam - One of the world's largest religions, brought into being in 622 AD by Mohammed who in middle-age became a prophet. Islam follows the worship of Although, one must be greatly knowledgeable in the religion of Islam and well-versed in the book of the Koran to really explain correctly, which the author is not.

J

Jack The Ripper - The Daily Express in 1931 ran a most interesting story that strongly indicated that Jack The Ripper had been named and his home pointed out to the police force of the day by Robert James Lees. This has never been completely accepted or completely disproved for that matter and remains a mystery to some extent.

Jainism - A religion of India, perhaps at one time closely related to the Hindu faith with aspects of Buddhism. Believed to have been brought into being by the teacher Vardhamana.

James, William - 1842-1910 A professor pf psychology at the Harvard University in America and an original member of the ASPR. A true believer in the occurrences of psychic phenomena James never, it is alleged, completely accepted the fact of spirit existence as tested and proven to his satisfaction.

Jeans, Dr Norman - Conducted tests on himself using differing anaesthetics to see if there would be the possibility of heightening psychic experiences. His research suggested that whilst inhaling nitrous oxide he could see or view remotely events and other places at great distance.

Joan of Arc (1411-1431) - The story of the Maid of Orleans and the voices in her head which advised her on personal aspects of her life and later advanced battle techniques to defeat France's enemies are well-reported in history. Of simple peasant stock her clairvoyant abilities were good enough to convince the Dauphin of her genuineness. Today she would surely be described as a most gifted medium.

Jehovah - The entity described as the spirit guide of Moses and advisor of the Jews during their times of passing through the wilderness.

Jehovah Witness - A religion whose belief is based in the literal word of the Bible and the acceptance that God's kingdom will come to those in this earth time and that the non-believers who are evil and wicked will be eliminated and destroyed.

Jesuit - A member of the order of the Society of Jesus, believed brought into being by Ignatius Loyola around 1534.

Jesus - Many Spiritualists have different views of how Jesus should be described or his life and times summarised. Almost all believe Jesus the Nazarene was a brilliant, if not the finest ever, medium, born of Jewish parentage and possibly trained as a Rabbi. Others claim he studied the doctrine of the Essenes in the early part of his life and then became a healer, teacher and proclaimer of how God would wish men and women to live. There is little doubt he had a huge following in the ancient lands of the Middle East but his outspoken open criticism of the more orthodox religions of the area he lived in possibly led people to consider him too much of a danger to be allowed to live. The whole basis of the Christian religion is resurrection. Some Spiritualists consider this a complete truth too, whereas other Spiritualists may feel Jesus materialised or appeared in Spirit, appropriate to their beliefs that such things did and can happen to this day. One must accept that Jesus was a Jew and may never have claimed to have founded any religion. The books of the New Testament are extremely enlightening but it is said there were other documents that were destroyed. All Spiritualists would say Jesus was a great teacher of how everyone's life and spiritual progression should be, working towards love for one another and peace and understanding of others.

Joire, Dr Paul - Was a professor of psychological instate of France and conducted important informative studies of psychical research and also hypnotism.

Jones, Dennis - MSNU. Public Relations Officer for the Spiritualists' National Union. Fine worker for Spiritualism generally.

Judge - Usually under test conditions an independent witness or tester who decides whether something is paranormal or normal.

Jung, Professor C. G. - One of the leading fathers of the knowledge of psychology whose work on symbolism, methods of divination, especially astrology and the I Ching, and meaningful coincidences makes him of great interest and still one of the most important sources of study for any parapsychologist or student of Spiritualism and mediumship to this day.

K

Ka - The Egyptian word for the etheric body or double that is spoken of in psychic and spiritualistic terms.

Kabbala - Ancient Jewish doctrine (see Cabbala).

Kama Rupa - A term in the Hindu religion for a sort of astral overcoat that may remain with the body after death that gradually disintegrates. Not accepted by Spiritualists really.

Kardec, Allan (1804-1869) - Member of the Society of Magnetism and important investigator of clairvoyance, trance mediumship and other areas of early Spiritualism. Published an important document called The Spirits' Book, described by Spiritualists today as the bible of Spiritualism.

Karma - The belief that what you give will be returned to you and what you fail to do will result in you receiving back the same. Perhaps originally part of the Buddhist religion and pathway which teaches 'what you sow you shall surely reap, therefore live your life planting good things, never bad'.

Karma Yoga - Pathway of study that should ultimately bring about total unselfishness to the individual.

Karter, Kathleen - New York based medium considered by many including famed parapsychologist, Professor Hans Holzer, as one of America's best mediums.

Key Cards - Some Psi tests require mediums and psychics to choose an individual card from perhaps three or five and achieve a 'better than average' result

Keys of the Tarot - This is the Major Arcana which consists of 22 cards. Very important and part of all proper tarot card packs.

Kilner, Dr Walter J. (1847-1920) - A major notary of St Thomas's Hospital, London. His experiments looking at and researching the human aura using what he called Dicyanin Dye

Screens, whereby the eyes and vision were claimed to be made more sensitive and capable of clearer vision psychically speaking, by looking through his screens and then looking at a living body in reduced light in front of a black backcloth. It was claimed by Kilner that aura bands could be seen by many people, not just sensitives, and that appropriate readings and correlations could be made.

Kilner Screen Goggles - The common name to describe Kilner's Screens manufactured in the smaller form of goggles, of a similar size to normal glasses.

King, John - Claimed to be the spirit guide of many mediums over the years, perhaps most famously recorded as working with the famed Davenport Brothers in the nineteenth century. Also claimed as a guide by Mme Blavatsky, Paladino and many mediums including one or two today.

King, Katie - Spirit guide of Florence Cook and interestingly suggested by several individuals in the Spiritualist movement at that time as being John King's daughter (see above).

Kirlian Photography - A special method of taking photos that used extremely high-frequency level electric currents. The apparatus was invented by Professor Kirlian of Russia and shows the life force or aura around many living things such as people's hands, leaves, plant life, etc.

Koan - A difficulty or great problem requiring deep thought and meditation. Usually founded in the practice of Zen Buddhism. Structured on the basis that an immediate impulse or idea gives the insight to that which at one time was considered unfathomable or unanswerable by the individual.

Krishna - A deity, god-figure, worshipped and revered across many traditions of Hinduism where he is usually seen as a young man in charge of a herd of cows sometimes playing a flute. Exemplified in the Bhagavata Purana or as a young prince offering wisdom and philosophy as exemplified in the Bhagavad Gita.

Kubler-Ross, Elizabeth - Dr Kubler-Ross is a very fine psychic researcher and also medical doctor. She has greatly helped people at the time of death and is convinced of the truth of life after death. She has written several books about the afterlife and should be given great acknowledgement for expressing views that not all the medical profession may agree with. All of her books should be of interest and researched by those interested in medical matters, death and the afterlife.

Kundalini - According to Eastern traditions and sometimes within Yoga kundalini is described as the deeply seated hidden psychic force and ability right at the base of the spine, some would say within the semen, which is dormant until activated through meditation and other techniques. An interest in this would require further study by the reader.

Lama - Tibetan Priest, follower of the doctrine of Buddhism.

Lang, Andrew (1843-1912) - Wrote extensively on anthropology, ghosts, hauntings, mythology and history. Also, propagated the study of scrying and dowsing and wrote an interesting study of the life and times of Joan of Arc exemplifying her time in this world from a mediumistic point of view.

Laws of Nature - Many Spiritualists do not believe in miracles, suggesting that all phenomena is relevant to natural laws and that what may seem miraculous in context of yesterday and today will be answered by science and Spiritualism in the future, though some Spiritualists do say miracles happen outside the laws of nature.

Laying on of Hands - Spiritual healing usually takes place by the healer's hands being applied to the recipient's physical body, though healing can happen without touch as in distant healing (see Distant Healing).

Leader, Circle - Most development circles have one person who is recognised as the circle leader. This can be the medium teacher or it can be someone of great experience and knowledge of Spiritualism such as in the field of philosophy in the religion. He or she must be very sensible, well-grounded and not show favouritism to any individual but rather concentrate on the progress of all within the circle.

Lees, Robert James - Highly acclaimed British medium and writer who was alleged to have been a confidante to Queen Victoria on several occasions. Lees was also claimed to be a very good healer who particularly excelled at diagnosis and according to some elements of the British media the man who found and named Jack the Ripper.

Leonard, Gladys Osborne - Veteran and early British medium. It is claimed that Raymond Lodge, the son of Sir Oliver Lodge, made his first communication to this world and his father through her mediumship after the First World War. Subject to many tests, Leonard was never proven to be anything but a fine instrument for Spirit.

Levitation - To raise or suspend a person or other object clearly off the floor without any human force, assistance, or equipment. Only very specially gifted mediums can achieve this.

Leylines - Some Spiritualists believe today there are alignments, patterns and very powerful earth energy systems that link together many ancient and sometimes sacred sites, such as stone circles, churches and other places of high spiritual or esoteric importance. In 1925 Alfred Watkins, who worked for the University of Cambridge at one time, published a book called The Old Straight Track claiming that many ancient sites were indeed connected by leys and leylines and also that a date could be placed on ancient sites and other buildings by dowsing them with a pendulum using varying lengths of cord.

Life - In simple terms the word used to describe any measured period of time in any example or item.

Life After Death - All Spiritualists believe there is life after death.

Life Review - An experience many claim to have just before death where the whole of their life experiences replay before them in their mind.

Light - Many mediums from the past insisted on demonstrating their gift in the dark or under subdued light. The author has always considered this an unfortunate requirement, opening the medium to claims of fraud, whether deserved or not, and not really required. However, some mediums do require this and in fact sudden or unexpected light occurring during a demonstration could cause illness or such a shock to the medium that varying levels of injury, including death, might happen. But mediums such as D. D. Homer, Paladino and some modern mediums today have demonstrated quite comfortably and well in bright daylight.

The Lights - Ancient astrological term from astrology

describing the sun and the moon,

Like Attracts Like - It is often said in Spiritualism that there is an important consideration when working as a medium or opening oneself up to Spirit when less experienced, that like attracts like. There is the possibility that the inexperienced sensitive might find unkind or unfriendly troublesome spirits drawn towards their vibration, and of course it is said that those who are evil, corrupt or unpleasant will not make good mediums!

Lily Dale - National Spiritualists Association of Churches. The main home of many Spiritualists in the United States. It can be found in the wider state of New York and is very much like a small village inhabited by Spiritualists from all over America and other parts of the world - some are actually residents. Contact them at NSAOC, PO Box 217, Lily Dale, NY 14752-0217, USA.

Limbo - Traditionally described as the place in-between worlds, perhaps best recognised by the Catholic religion, where sinners are sent to find themselves when Heaven is not open to them. This is a view not shared as being a truth by Spiritualists and Spiritualism.

Lincoln, Abraham - One of the most famous of America's presidents and claimed to be more than interested in Spiritualism. There are even claims that his insistence that slavery would be abolished was after he had received spirit guidance though mediums of the day, Nettie Colburn and others.

Locke, John (1632-1704) - British academic and philosopher of the Empirist School. He studied human understanding and put forward the view there was a relationship between philosophy and metaphysics that should be considered appropriately.

Lodge, Sir Oliver, FRCS, D.Sc, LI.D, MA (1851-1940) - Great pioneer of Spiritualism, helped to develop radio. Physicist, highly respected professor in several fields and one of the most respected of scientists of his generation. Much can be read of his son Raymond contacting him from the spirit world. One of the very first scientists to write about subatomic particles and their relevance to the spirit world. He also helped many mediums and Spiritualism itself to progress.

Lord's Prayer, The - Considered one of the oldest of prayers, which Christians claim was given to the disciples through Jesus' mission on Earth, although it may be grounded in older Jewish roots, with the possibility of it's originally coming into being in Babylon. Evidence for this is found in a relic discovered in 1882 that seems to suggest the same context of wording. The Jewish people may have learned it in ancient Chaldaic, a form of communication they would have learned during their time of enslavement to the ancient Babylonians.

Lost Abilities - There are times when many mediums have the experience of losing their abilities for a short while and it is sometimes said that this can be part of a learning curve, making the medium clearly realise that they are an instrument for Spirit and cannot rely on their own abilities. Mediumship gifts almost always return to those who wish to work for Spirit.

Lost Spirits - A term often used to describe discarnate entities who have remained close to the earth plane by refusing to accept what they are or that they have passed through the physical death state. Acceptance usually happens when so-called lost spirits have their position explained to them by a rescue medium or rescue circle.

Lotus Position - The cross-legged meditative position taken up by parishioners of yoga with the intention of stilling the mind, relaxing the body and bringing about complete awareness or in the advanced state raising the kundalini condition or stimulating the chakra centres (see Kundalini and Chakra Centres).

Lotus Sutra - In classical Buddhist pathways the transcendent Gotama speaks from a high position (mountain perhaps) of the wisdom and understanding of the cosmic Buddha, enlightenment and the reason for everything that can ever be (see Buddhism, and read about Gotama for further study and knowledge).

Lourdes - A place in France claimed to be a site for miraculous cures. In 1858, Mary the mother of Jesus is claimed to have presented herself to Bernadette Soubiros, a young girl suffering from disability, in a nearby cave. Since that time many have reported having been to this area and receiving healing either immediately or shortly afterwards. Spiritualists would probably say that the healing received by people suggests ongoing spirit assistance because of the apparition involved. Those of a traditional Western religion, and other religions, might claim faith is required to be helped at Lourdes. Spiritualists and others would not agree with this.

Lower Astral Plane - Describes the first level of existence where people from this world who have much to learn, such as murderers, cruel and wicked people, move to after their physical death.

Lucid Dream - This is a dream in which the individual has some awareness and understanding that they are dreaming and retain some control over what they are dreaming about.

Lucidity - A descriptive word which means a knowledge of that which is considered supernatural or supernormal but which with experience and training can be learned, such as clairvoyance, or even psychometry, amongst other things.

Luminous Body - A term Pythagoras used for what is known in Spiritualist terms as the astral body.

Luminous Phenomena - Linked with physical mediumship, this is the substance that emanates from the medium and is a little bit like the type of light that is seen in insects that shine in the dark. It sometimes smells similar to phosphorus and in more modern times cleaning fluid such as Ajax.

Lycanthropy - An old belief that human beings can under certain situations transform themselves into materialised animal shapes, particularly that of a wolf. Sometimes described as shape-shifting. Some have even suggested that this may have associated links to the non-native black cats claimed to be roaming the wilds of Britain. Most Spiritualists would consider this to be extremely unlikely, if not a completely ridiculous theory.

M

MacDonald - The guide of the modern-day medium Philip Solomon.

MacLaine, Shirley - Great worker whose foray into Spiritualism and New Age practices came to the fore when her book Out On A Limb, was published in 1983. The American film star has been a great facilitator in bringing many new ideas from the psychic realm and particularly past-life awareness possibilities to the general public. She is the sister of another famous film star, Warren Beatty.

Macro-PK - A psycho-kinetic experience that can actually be seen or experienced rather than simply described.

Magi - The word Magi is always associated with the Three Wise Men but is also an ancient description for the academic or learned classes of Medes and Persia, usually priests from Mesopotamia.

Magic - White magic is generally practiced by those who follow the Wiccan religion, witches and warlocks, and is usually closely associated to healing. Black Magic is where individuals look for supernatural assistance with evil intentions usually towards others.

Magicians - Illusionists and those who entertain by sleight of hand.

Magnetic Healing - Can best be described as an alternative healing practice that some believe comes about because magnetic fields have healing powers. In the eighteenth century Mesmer, for instance, claimed that Maximillian Hell, a Jesuit priest, showed him how people could be cured of many ailments with a magnetic steel plate. It is alleged Mesmer copied Hell's magnetic therapy and that it may have been the first example of magnetic healing that is known of. Today many people claim benefits from wearing magnets close to the skin and body and they are sold by various companies throughout the world.

Magnetic Phenomena - The medium Henry Slade was well-known for moving the needle of a compass or other pointing instrument, such as needles, by the will of the mind.

Magnetometer - A piece of paper attached to cord in a glass cylinder made to move by thought power to a measured distance. A test for the paranormal.

Magus - The guide and control of the Reverend Stainton Moses, Moses believed Magus had lived a life as an African of importance many thousands of years ago, but was never given this information from the guide himself.

Magnus - The guide and control of the modern day medium Colin Fry.

Mahabharata - Indian Sanskrit poems expressing the view that the god, Vishnu, was incarnated for men and women's benefit in the person of Mahabharata, a charioteer, and Krishna as Rama, a legendary king and hero.

Mahatma - An ancient word that means great or marvellous soul in simple translation as in the Mahatma Ghandi.

Mahayana - A large division from the Buddhist doctrine.

Mahdi - A messiah to come in the future from the religion of Islam.

Man - The whole of the human race. Spiritualists tend to talk of human kind which is more appropriate and politically correct.

Mana - The Maori tribe of New Zealand used this word to describe mystical or magical powers, which may be better described as paranormal forces.

Manichaeism - An ancient Gnostic religion.

Manning, Matthew - Born 1955. Psychic and healer. Also writer of numerous books on the paranormal. Claimed that he and his family suffered poltergeist activity at his home in Cambridge, which continued during his education at Oakham School. Much investigation of Matthew's experiences were undertaken by Dr George Owen from the Cambridge Psychical Research Society and later outlined in a book called The Link. Manning today spends a lot of his time in Suffolk and gives his greatest attention to psychic healing. Also claimed artistic ability inspired through the spirit influence of Pablo Picasso and others.

Mantra - A form prayer or chanting once only common to eastern religions and faith, popularised in the west in the New Age Movement and practised by some Spiritualists today.

Mantra Yoga - Realisation of oneself through prayer or chanting.

Manu - A term for a master or wise one more relevant to the occult than Spiritualism.

Many Mansions - The seven levels of higher existence to many Spiritualists.

Marryat, Florence (1837-1899) - Author who wrote several books about Spiritualism. Was a capable medium herself and promoted many of the mediums of those days.

Mass Hypnosis - Where large groups, even nations, have claimed to be under the power of one individual to be influenced to do his or her will.

Master - A word often used in the past to describe a teacher. Spiritualists today do not tend to speak of masters, rather respecting all.

Match - Another word to describe accepted evidence between medium and sitter (see Hit).

Matching Test Results - Where two sensitives being tested both achieve the same result such as in naming a specific card, etc.

Material - Mediums will often speak of material conditions, which really means the ordinary everyday physical matters of living your life in this world.

Materialisation - Where spirits form with some solidity, are reasonably visible, and can be recognised as a normal human shape.

Materialism - A term which describes and includes everything to be material in context with no spiritual influence.

Matter - The substance which all physical objects are made up of and constitutes the universe as it is understood and observed at this time within science. It might be easy to consider manifestations of energy matter like light and sound as not really material, but according to the law of relativity energy and matter can be converted into one another and matter is said to have mass that occupies space. Further reading in physics is suggested for those interested in more than just a simple explanation of matter.

McKenzie, J. Hewat (1870-1929) - Founder of the British College of Psychic Science. Lecturer and researcher of all matters psychical, particularly promoted the work of lady mediums Gladys Osborne Leonard and Eileen Garrett.

Mean Chance Expectation (MCE) - The expected chance result, generally in a psi experiment.

Medicine Man - Generally priests and healers who are almost certainly natural mediums who conducted religious ceremonies and advised the tribes of the native American Indians. Considered to be some of the first known of Spiritualist mediums.

Medicine Woman - Exactly the same role as a medicine man (see Medicine Man).

Meditation - A mental state when the mind blocks out outer influences and focuses on one important matter. It is used to progress psychic and mediumistic ability and taught in many Spiritualist development classes as a way to quieten the mind and focus on your work as an instrument for Spirit.

Medium - An individual who has the ability to link between the spirit world and the physical world to prove to others the continuing existence of life after death.

Mediumship - The practice of a Spiritualist medium when giving messages between the two worlds.

Medium Coeli - In astrology this describes an important part of an individual's horoscope, perhaps better known as the 'Midheaven'.

Mediumistic Development - Those who are sensitive to spirit can train their mediumistic development in a Spiritualist church, open circles, closed circles and by further training and study, such as at the Spiritualist college of Arthur Findley in Essex and with other organisations.

Memory - Basically the part of the mind that can bring forth and recall all that is learned and impressions that have been picked up.

Memory, Cosmic - Some Spiritualists believe there is a sort of university of memory which can be consulted during the right trance states. It may help to read around the cosmic consciousness or see the entry for 'Akashic Records'.

Mental Illness Healing - Many people with mental illness or psychological conditions have been helped by spiritual healing. Some Spiritualists believe that when the balance of the mind is correct a lot of natural healing takes place also.

Mentalism - A word to describe magic as practised by a magician or conjurer. Not part of Spiritualism.

Mental Mediumship - This is where the guide or spirit the medium links with controls the medium's subconscious mind and uses the physical body as an instrument of communication, sometimes expression and action. This is also known as physical mediumship.

Mental Radio - Some individuals have the belief that spirit messages can be picked up by using radio receivers as a tool for communication from the other side. Also the space between radio stations, a sort of buzz, has been recorded and claimed by some to include messages from incarnate spirits, exemplified to some extent in the film White Noise.

Mesmer, Franz Anton (1734-1815) - Austrian by birth, he believed in animal magnetism, a term that was later to be seen as the forerunner to mesmerism and hypnotism.

Mesmerism - Famed German doctor Franz Mesmer claimed mesmerism could be used in healing and had many other benefits to mankind. Hypnotism and hypnotherapy, which developed from his work, are now certainly used by some Spiritualists who believe in regression and past lives, and is also used by the medical profession in doctors' surgeries, clinics and hospitals.

Messages - The word that describes information given to Spirit from the other side then passed to those in this world.

Messiah - The Jewish name for The Anointed One. In Christianity always associated with Jesus Christ.

Metagraphology - A word to describe analysing a person's handwriting using psychic ability such as that of a psychometrist. Otto Reimann was one of the original users and a respected historical figure in what is now a very popular form of character analysis.

Metal Bending - Some psychics such as Uri Geller claim an ability to produce energy just from thought, which will bend metal such as spoons, knives and forks.

Metamorphosis - Meaning shape-shifting. Some people, as an example, might change from a human form to that of an animal.

Metaphysics - A study which looks to understand and find answers to things that are believed to exist but as yet have no complete measurable answer as to whether they do. Generally studied academically both objectively and subjectively.

Metempsychosis - Another word for reincarnation.

Meyers, Ethel Johnson - Highly respected medium and psychic who was invited to work with parapsychologist Professor Hans Holzer to investigate the famous alleged haunted house, Amityville, as part of the defence case of Ronnie DeFeo at his trial for multiple murders at the house, on the instruction of his acting attorney, William Webber.

Micro-PK - Psycho-kinetic effects that cannot be clearly witnessed or supported but are claimed through wider analysis.

Mind - The thinking faculty.

Mind Cure - A term brought into being by Phineas Quinby, an American of the nineteenth century and practitioner of mesmerism, which claims that the mind can cure any condition. An important person for Spiritualists to study. Some Spiritualists believe perfect balance of the mind also cures all ailments.

Mind Reading - A belief outside the religion of Spiritualism that some mediums use a form of mind reading or telepathy and then replay this to the individual as if it was a message from spirits on the other side.

Ministry of Angels - The ministry of angels is acknowledged by Spiritualists through communion with spirits, and perhaps particularly in the context of healing, which at many times may seem to miraculously come from above but is truly understood and accepted by those who understand Spiritualism.

Minor Arcana - The 56 cards and suits of the standard Tarot pack.

Mirabelli, Carmine (1889-1950) - Spiritist medium of Brazil.

Extensively tested by numerous scientists, many claimed his psychic abilities were entirely genuine at a time and place in history where there must have been many who would question such gifts. Mirabelli's abilities stood up well to such tests.

Miracles - Events or happenings which are considered super-natural or supernormal.

Misdirection - The skill of the conjurer, sleight of hand. This has nothing to do with Spiritualism.

Miss - The failure to have a message from the other side accepted by a reader or someone in a church congregation.

Mnemonist - An individual who has acquired and learned methods to expand and create a vast amount of memory ability.

Mohammed - The original founder and of course prophet of the religion of Islam.

Monition - A warning from the spirit world or the outlining of some event that has happened or will come to be and that is not of this world.

Montgomery, Ruth Shick (1912-2001) - American journalist and Christian psychic similar to Edgar Cayce and Jeane Dixon and protégé of Arthur Ford. She believed she had a mission to educate the people in this world to believe in life after death. She also believed in reincarnation and suggested that many physical and mental illnesses and conditions were relevant to difficulties people had had in past lives. In the States a founder member of the Association for Past Life Research and Therapy, she was also the author of many books of a Spiritualist nature and in many ways considered important in the New Age society that came to the fore in the 70s and 80s. Montgomery also claimed in some of her writings that she had lived at the time of Jesus Christ and people at that time would have known her as Mary the sister of Lazarus. She also made many predictions, several of which were claimed to have been proven accurate.

Mormons - In 1830 Joseph Smith founded the church of Jesus Christ of Latter Day Saints, after being given a revelation spiritually suggesting information on the lost tribes of the Jewish people, who according to some legends found their way to America. The Mormons settled and grew as a community in Salt Lake City, Utah. They set their own regulations and laws, which included polygamy.

Morris, Meurig - A British lady medium also considered an excellent speaker, she became known in Spiritualism for her efforts to produce a powerful spirit voice projected through the Columbia gramophone machine of its day.

Morse, J. J. (1848-1919) - Brilliant British medium of limited academic tutoring, yet when inspired through trance spoke eloquently and philosophically on many subjects including the philosophy of Spiritualism. He also acted as editor in chief of Spiritualist newspapers and generally promoted the religion very well.

Moses, Rev. William Stainton (1839-1892) - One of the major names of Spiritualism, yet a minister of the Church of England. He attained an MA from Oxford and was the editor of Light. Under the pseudonym of M. A. Oxon, he penned the important Spirit Teachings, which in its day was considered the bible of Spiritualism.

Mother Shipton (1488-1561) - Ursula Southill, better known as Mother Shipton, was an English soothsayer and alleged prophetess. She claimed to have made many incredible predictions, such as the coming of the Great Plague of London, the dispatch of the Spanish Armada and its defeat and the Great Fire of London. She was claimed to be the daughter of Agatha Southill, herself considered an incredibly wise woman or witch of her times. One prediction she made that proved inaccurate was that the world would end in 1881. Some researchers have since claimed that the written records referred to with regard to Mother Shipton may have been nineteenth-century forgeries

Movement of Objects - The correct name for movement of objects by paranormal or psychic efforts is known as telekinesis.

Moyes, Winifred - Credited with many of the teachings and outlines set out for the Greater World Christian Spiritualist movement. Her guide was known as Zodiac, and the church claims Jesus Christ as its sole leader, which is not the position with other Spiritualist churches such as the SNU.

Muir, Gaye - An excellent medium of international renown. A fantastic worker for Spirit whose energy to travel and demonstrate mediumship does not seem to have reduced as she has got older. An author of good books for anyone interested in mediumship or developing in the Spiritualist religion. She often describes quite clearly two levels of existence: the present that we are living in now, and the second one that awaits us after our life on earth and death in this world. A good teacher and helper of many of the young mediums practising today and a very fine worker for Spirit.

Multiple Personality - A condition psychiatrists diagnose in people who have inherent separate personalities that come to the consciousness and take that individual over.

Music - There are numerous instances in the history of Spiritualism and mediumship of music being played that is alleged to come from the spirit world itself or be produced by incarnate entities. Some mediums such as the author, feel they have been taught to play instruments and music through spirit inspiration rather than through traditional tuition in music.

Music of the Spheres - Pythagoras suggested there was a mathematical relationship that was musical in context and played between the planets or spheres.

Myers, Frederick William Henry (1843-1901) - Was one of the early pioneers of real psychical research. An academic scholar and poet, he was one of the early founders of the SPR, president in 1900. He worked with many famous mediums and was considered to have communicated to this world on his passing through the automatist Geraldine Cummins.

Mystic - An individual who has apparent mystical wisdom. Many from the New Age movement may have at one time described all healers, mediums and psychics, incorrectly really, as mystics.

Mysticism - A knowledge of God and the spirit world, perhaps attained by meditation and contemplation. Such knowledge is received and learned from other sources rather than through the normal senses or through academic study.

National Federation of Spiritual Healers (NFSH) - Brought into being in 1954 by a coming together of several healers associations, all with the common good and intent to bring healing and balance to all who ask of it.

National Laboratory of Psychical Research (NLPR) - Formed by the famous ghost hunter Harry Price in 1925 to look at every area of psychic phenomena. Price's investigation of Borley Rectory is considered a classic record of a haunted house.

National Spiritualists Association of Churches (NSAC) - The NSAC is the largest and oldest organisation in the United States of its kind for modern Spiritualism, first coming into being in 1893.

National Spiritualist Union (NSU) - Responsible for the majority of Spiritualist churches in the UK, education, training, and the financial aspects of the union and many other responsibilities.

Natural Philosophy - Now more applicably considered as physics.

Nature Spirits - Spirits of the earth which some sensitive people claim to have seen. In Ireland they may be described as the 'little people'. Some people at the height of New Age interest considered nature spirits to be part of a multi-spirit community such as an elemental spirit considered to have control and influence over natural forces.

Near Death Experience (NDE) - People that have been very close to death or actually described as being dead have experienced going down a tunnel with a light at the end. Reaching the light they often see loved ones from the other side and have been given the choice to stay with them or return to complete more tasks in this life. Often life-changing for those who have experienced it.

Necromancy - Conjuring of the dead. Much more applicable to black magic. Spiritualists would wholeheartedly claim that such an action is not possible and would have no wish to try to achieve such a thing.

Negative and Positive - Terms sometimes used by Spiritualists to exemplify perhaps a negative or positive link that may be received from the spirit world, negative not really having any meaning, positive giving specific evidence of the identity of an incarnate personality.

Neil, Sharon - Belfast born, this Irish medium is unusual because she is one of the few practising blind mediums. This has not affected her abilities and she is noted for her accurate messages. She has also written books, appeared on a TV documentary and toured the UK demonstrating her gifts.

Nerve Aura - Words used by Dr Rhodes Buchanan to explain the psychometric faculty relevant to the aura he suggested could be seen by suitable sensitives.

New Age - A term popular in the 1980s encompassing a wide area of beliefs such as mysticism, some areas of the occult, rein-carnation, ecology, parapsychology and Spiritualism, alongside adherence to many complementary medicinal practices and healing techniques. The New Age belief and its practices in many ways grew up in the West but also encompassed many Eastern traditions. Its early roots can be traced back to social situations and political changes of the 1960s considered unfair. Sir George Trevalion is considered by some to be the father figure of the modern New Age movement as we understand it today.

Newspaper Test - A test designed by those who wish to have spirit messages proven. It makes the use of telepathy impossible. Names and dates are marked out in various columns of not yet published newspapers and the medium is required to predict the news in advance. Remarkable results were claimed especially through the mediumship of Mrs Osborne Leonard.

Nictalopes - Term for an individual claimed to have the ability to see quite clearly in total darkness.

Nirvana - The equivalent of heaven in various Eastern traditions, religions and pathways.

Noah's Ark Society, The - A society that specialised in the promotion and development of physical mediumship. In recent years one of its well-known developed physical mediums was Colin Fry, also known as Lincoln, who brought through the words of his spirit guide Magnus on many occasions. The society closed down but is possibly to re-open in the future.

Northage, Ivy (1909-2002) - For close on 40 years Ivy Northage served at the Spiritualist Association of Great Britain. Her lectures and teaching abilities were considered to be of the very highest standard. She wrote some excellent books alongside her study courses. One of her best-known and most useful books for any Spiritualist is called While I Remember. Ivy is also widely credited with being the inspiration for some of today's best young mediums and was considered an extremely accurate medium herself, working with Chan, her spirit guide. Some of her wonderful lectures were recorded and are available for people today. A fine worker who gave great service to Spiritualism.

Nostradamus, Michael de (1503-1556) - French psychic, astrologer and physician, Nostradamus possessed superb mind and reasoning abilities. He became an advisor to King Henry II and Charles IX. Around 1550 he collectively produced and presented his written predictions of what was to come, known as the 'quatrains', all in coded messages and stories. Many of his predictions are claimed to have come true throughout history and are still attaining fulfilment in the modern age.

Numerology - The study of the meaning and predictive possibility of numbers.

Oaten, Ernest - One-time president of the Spiritualists National Union with a similar post taken up for the National Spiritualists' Federation. A highly capable author and writer in many areas of psychic phenomena in the 1920s and 30s.

OBE - Out-of-body experience where someone senses themselves looking down on the physical body and still sensing a connection to that body (see Astral Travel).

Object Reading - A word that really belongs to the field of psychometry (see Psychometry).

O'Brien, Stephen - Highly respected Spiritualist medium, author of numerous best-selling books, self-help tapes and a respected healer too. Has also written many spiritual and other articles of a teaching nature in a career approaching 30 years serving Spirit.

Obsession - May be seen as a cornerstone of religious activity within Spiritism. Defined by Allan Kardec to mean the interference of a subjugating spirit upon a weaker one and taken for granted as meaning negative influence of the spirit of an evil deceased person upon the mind of one that is still alive (and sometimes vice versa). May be considered by Spiritists as quite dangerous for the unprepared or untrained medium, but sometimes has to be faced. Claimed to be one of the most frequent causes of mental illness and criminal or anti-social behaviour. Often treated at Spiritist centres through teaching, explanation and prayer.

Occultism - Practices that are involved with the secret powers of mind and spirit. Many ancient traditions were part of occult practices, almost all searching for knowledge that is hidden or forbidden in some contexts. A Spiritualist should be looking to offer service to his or her fellow men and women rather than for personal physical or spiritual gains.

O'Keeffe, Dr. Ciarán - Became known for covering the para-psychology angle on the popular TV ghost hunting series, *Most Haunted*.

Old Soul - These words have long had special meaning for many groups. Some Spiritualists believe that many lives are lived in this world and on other levels of existence, working ultimately with the closeness of the godhead. They may speak of an old soul in the context of an ancient life lived. A lot of Spiritualists do not support this view or opinion.

O'Leary, Laurie - Promoter and manager of the two Doris's, firstly Doris Stokes and then Doris Collins. A man who also helped to bring many young mediums to the notice of the media and the general public.

Olga - The guide of Rudi Schneider.

Olshaker, Edward - A serious researcher and long-term freelance writer whose work has been commissioned and appeared in many publications, particularly in America, for major organisations such as the New York Times and others. A book of particular interest to Spiritualists is his book Witness to the Unsolved, whereby some of the world's famous mediums have investigated and reported on the unusual deaths of some very major celebrities. The British medium selected for this book was Philip Solomon.

Om - An ancient word believed to have special significance when sounded or chanted, possibly of ancient Sanskrit origin.

Omens - Signs that suggest or foretell what is to come.

Om Nai Padme Hum - One of the most famous of chanted Mantras and considered by many to bring about spiritual progression and grounding often before receiving great spiritual wisdom.

Omnipotent - Descriptive word that may be used to describe God, the Almighty, or All Powerful Being.

Omniscient - Knowledge of all things, total wisdom, god-like wisdom.

OOBE - Out of body experiences (see Out of Body Experience).

Open Circle - This is usually a circle in a Spiritualist church where individuals can sit for development, often open to anyone. Sometimes a facility just for church members, it is the first stage of all mediumistic development.

Opposition - Generally a term used in astrology when two things, such as planets, etc. would be opposed to each other.

Oracle - Generally a shrine that also has healing or predictive powers, such as Aphrodites' Spring in Cyprus.

Order of the Knights Templar - The Knights Templar were soldiers and also a religious order who travelled to the Holy Land during the time of the Crusades with their claimed intention to protect pilgrims. The founders were Geoffrey de Saint-Homer and Hugh de Payns, who established a religious order on the ancient site of Solomon's Temple. The Templars attracted many noblemen and became fierce in battle and incredibly wealthy, so much so that in 1307 Philip V of France, claimed to be in serious debt to the Templars, denounced them as immoral and heretics and was alleged to put in place a plan to eliminate them completely from the face of the earth. Legend has it that many Templars escaped and founded organisations such as the Order of the Rosy Cross, or the Rosicrucians, and the Freemasons. Modern legends in books such as Dan Brown's The Da Vinci Code suggest they may have had incredible links to Jesus living and surviving in Europe. Many Spiritualists have taken an interest in the Knights Templar and feel there is a story set to be told.

Orgone Energy - An energy force described by Wilhelm Reich to exemplify the universal life form, closely linked to sex and sexuality.

Ouija Board - A combination of two European words, French 'Oui' and the German 'Ja', which unusually both mean 'yes'. It is a wooden board which has a plain pointer or glass that people place a finger on. The pointer is then, allegedly under spirit influence, pushed towards letters of the alphabet which are usually around the outside. In the wrong or inexperienced hands, especially where an individual with latent mediumistic ability is present, it can be a very dangerous item. Many people have been terrified after receiving messages, possibly from the first level of existence, from spirits who would enjoy scaring or joking with people in a most horrible way, in just the sort of way someone of that personality would have done in their earthly life.

Ortzen, Tony - The former editor of Psychic News, the oldest and most respected and established newspaper of its kind in the world today. Tony, alongside Gary Johnson, also edits and runs Two Worlds magazine. Tony has been involved in paranormal and psychical research for over 30 years, has worked alongside some of the most famous mediums in the world, and has interviewed many of the top mediums and psychics too, whilst also acting as consultant or advisor to many media and publishing companies.

Overshadowing - This is where a medium is controlled by a spirit, but probably only with quite light physical influence, i.e. some similarities to a spirit's voice or perhaps features. Occurs particularly when part of the early development of transfiguration mediumship.

Oversoul - In simple explanation, the higher self. For more formal understanding study of the Hindu or Brahma caste system may be helpful to the reader.

Owen, Robert Dale (1801-1877) - Great humanist who wrote some good books relevant to the early development of Spiritualism.

Pacifist - One who opposes violence and aggression. All true Spiritualists are advised that this pathway is part of their progression and aim to achieve such attitudes in this life.

Painting, Psychic - Many psychic individuals have produced quite remarkable paintings. These people have often claimed to have no artistic ability and are influenced by incarnate spirits. Some mediums who are also psychic artists produce likenesses on canvas and other surfaces of people's loved ones on the other side.

Paladino, Eusapia (1854-1918) - Considered one of the best European physical mediums, discovered by Signor Damini through the spirit messages of John King, who passed the information back. Eusapia was his reincarnated daughter in our world.

Palmistry - Should really be called Chiromancy. Some practitioners claim to be able to comment on the character of an individual and even predict their life potential from the lines upon their palms. Not generally considered a form of mediumship in the strictest sense.

Paraesthesia - A sensation of tingling or slight shaking that some mediums say they feel as they are about to link with their guide.

Paranoia - a mental illness that often includes imagined situations and hallucinations. Not at all similar to clairvoyance and clairaudience, which some psychiatrists have claimed may have similarities.

Paranormal - Something that is outside of normal or present scientific knowledge. Paranormal matters are of great interest to Spiritualists.

Parapsychology - The word was first used by J. B. Rhine with regard to his work and research of paranormal phenomena, although today we would more likely speak of psychical research. Many modern parapsychologists such as Professor Hans Holzer of New York are open-minded and support the existence of spirit life. Others tend to still search for more 'normal' answers alongside the paranormal.

Past Life Memories - Some Spiritualists claim they have clear memories of past life experiences and past lives. Also in reincarnation. Others such as the medium Colin Fry, completely refute such beliefs.

Past Life Regression - Many people have been taken back to other lives using methods such as meditation and hypnotherapy.

Pendulum - This is an object used by psychics and some dowsers. In its basic form a simple weight held by a cord. Some people, such as the academic Tom Lethbridge, have suggested the length of cord used is important in relation to what is searched for or asked for. Some Spiritualists, and more appropriately psychics, use pendulums to dowse for positions and places on maps to find objects and even for locating imbalance and illnesses in human beings. Other Spiritualists may say it is just a focus and that it is spirit influence that guides the response the pendulum gives.

Pentecost - Whit Sunday or Whitsun is probably one of the most important days to Christian Spiritualists in the United Kingdom. It is symbolically related to the Jewish festival of Shavuot which celebrates the descent of the Holy Spirit to the Apostles and other followers of Jesus, as it is described in the Book of Acts, Chapter 2.

Perception Circle - This is generally a development circle for those who are very new to Spiritualism, who may be considered as beginners who must be taught the basic philosophy of the religion of Spiritualism and how to prepare to receive and give simple messages to others in a proper and professional way. They must also be taught to use proper psychic protection in opening and closing down.

Percipient - He or she who receives or is given a telepathic message or other form of psychic communication.

Percussion - In séances of yesteryear, many sitters would listen for knocks, table raps and noises, sometimes with a coded message from the other side that would be known to a member of the séance. Victorian mediums claimed that the tapping noises were made by sticks formed from their ectoplasm that were capable of percussive noises or bangs, generally on the table they sat round.

Personality - The conscious and unconscious aspects that make everyone different and quite unique.

Peters, Alfred Vout - British medium respected at home and abroad and claimed to have worked with Sir Oliver Lodge on occasions. Perhaps best known for using psychometry to suggest the contents of Joanna Southcott's box, some say before it was later opened.

Phantasm - Another word for an apparition or vision.

Phantasmata - A word used in some movements for thought forms that can be passed between two or more people and proven correct and vice versa.

Phenomena of Spiritualism - According to man's belief, he would not be able to give a reasonable account of Spiritualism because any test or research would tend to be governed or painted by his or her own belief. You cannot know for sure until the effect, or death if you like, comes to give proof of the phenomena. Spiritualists believe emphatically in life after the physical death of this world.

Phenomenology - When an individual searches for the under-standing and meaning of an event, course of action, or phenomenon they have experienced.

Philosophy - The study of all physical, spiritual and mental phenomena and its understanding and meaning, as in the philosophy of Spiritualism.

Philosophy of Spiritualism - The philosophy of Spiritualism can be found within the words of the Seven Principles (see Seven Principles).

Photography, Psychic - Pictures of anything of a paranormal nature, ghosts, spectres and spirits.

Phrenology - The study of the shape and bumps of the human head with the inherent belief that capabilities, intelligence and lifetime potentials are there to be felt upon the human skull. Not considered mediumistic in context.

Physical Circles - The physical circle is only ever specifically for the development of one medium. In many cases it is operated in a darkened room with a red light as a minor illumination. The physical circle is quite similar to a controlled circle but it is hoped that as part of the development the medium concerned will be able to help bring about the manifestation of spirit presences and other physical phenomena. A great deal of work and development is needed to develop a true physical medium.

Physical Medium - This is a medium who can produce ectoplasm which can then be formulated by spirit influence into recognisable forms and shapes.

Physical Phenomena - This is the production of ectoplasm that can be used for materialisation. It also covers telekinesis with the requirement that physical phenomena on its own is not total proof of survival. This must be presented and shown in a recognisable semi-solid form supported by evidence of the spirit's personality.

Physics - A science that examines non-chemical properties of matter.

Pink - When seen in the aura pink is often associated with love.

Piper, Mrs Leonore E. (1859-1950) - An American trance medium from Boston. Considered by many to be possibly one of the finest mediums the States produced. Endorsed by Sir Oliver Lodge, Professor J. Hyslop and many other academic and intellectual investigators of psychical matters.

PK - Psycho-Kinesis (see Psycho-Kinesis).

Placebo Effect - Some parapsychologists say that spiritual healing happens to individuals simply because they believe in the treatment, claiming that some doctors and physicians have given tablets with no medical content at all to patients (a placebo pill) and the patient has improved or indeed got better, and that this healing is psychological in context.

Platt, Frau Lotte - Dutch psychic and psychometrist claimed to be one of the first people of such gifts to be used by a modern police force, mostly in Germany.

Planchette - A small board on casters or runners with a pen or pencil fixed to it with the intention that when a medium places his or her hand on the equipment it will write messages or draw pictures from incarnate bodies.

Planes - Different levels of existence in the higher life.

Planet, Information - Many individuals claim they have had intelligent communication from life forms on other planets, either through astral travel or communication similar to that received from the spirit world clairaudiently. Swedenborg expressed his interest in this area and therefore brings an authoritative interest to this field. Some Spiritualists believe in extra-terrestrial life and some don't.

Plato - A Greek philosopher who spent much of his life trying to find the answer to perfect life for the individual and altruism for others, a philosophy perhaps taken on board by those truly wishing to be Spiritualists.

Pneumatographer - One who is a medium for writing inspired from Spirit.

Pocomania - A Spiritist religion more common to the West Indies with some aspects of Voodoo (see Voodoo).

Poltergeist - A mischievous Spirit or entity which physically throws objects around, makes unusual noises and bangs, even on some occasions alleged to have started fires or plumbing floods by separating pipes, etc. The phenomena can generally be linked to a teenager going through the stages of puberty. In some instances other causes may be to blame.

Polytheism - He or she who accepts several gods rather than just one deity.

Portal - A doorway or gateway between the spirit world and the earth plane.

Possession - Whereby an individual is taken control of by Spirit or an unknown entity generally without their knowledge and permission.

Post-Cognitive Telepathy - A person might cognise accurately with another person, spirit, etc., enough times to be obviously outside of chance expectation. If it is clear that no other form of communication would be possible between them by any normal sensory means, then this could be described as post-cognitive telepathy.

Post-Mortem Message - Where a message has been written by a deceased person, secreted or locked away, which is then found, read and considered to be accurate (following a message from that person's spirit on the other side).

Power - A word that describes the various abilities that might be exemplified by an individual through any psychic or mediumistic ability.

Prãna - A special energy related to breathing that the eastern tradition believes is all around us and can be produced and attuned to with certain breathing techniques that are beneficial to mankind.

Prayer - A communication usually on a mental level sent out to higher spirit levels/God.

Precognition - To see a future event before it happens. To dream precognitively would be to dream of something that comes to be.

Prediction - To foretell that which is to come, often practised by fortune tellers and only very rarely by mediums.

Pre-Life Existence - It is a point of disagreement between many Spiritualists whether some live lives before and after their existence in this world. Some Spiritualists say definitely yes and some say definitely no.

Premonition - To predict with some detail what will happen in the near future. You may see, sense or dream this. The possibility of coincidence or chance must always be considered and premonitions should be written down whenever possible to be looked at more objectively later.

Presence - When one feels that something is close, such as a spirit or entity. Spiritualists may describe that as sensing a presence.

Price, Harry - Probably the most famous ghost hunter of them all. Author of many books and very early media presenter. Conducted the infamous investigations of Borley Rectory, claimed by many to be the most haunted house in the world.

Private Sitting - This is where an individual arranges to have a reading with a medium or possibly psychic with an agreed fee to be paid to the medium for their time and work. No true medium can guarantee what is hoped for from the other side and cannot contact anyone specifically in the Spirit world. In fact, it is always the Spirit world, only if they wish, who contact us, never the other way round.

Probability Effect - When a medium or psychic is tested for their ability and an average result is attained it is considered part of the probability effect.

Progression - The life pathway of every person through changes and experiences which bring learning and wisdom which prepares you for the next. Progression is also said to continue through several other higher levels of existence with the hope of ultimately becoming a perfectly developed spirit of the highest level.

Proof - This is a key word in Spiritualism. It is the job of all mediums to give information from the other side that proves without a shadow of a doubt that life hereafter is a fact.

Prophesy - Where someone makes a claim that something usually quite significant to mankind will happen in the future.

Prophet - In religion a prophet is an individual who encounters the divine, and receives important information for mankind to pass on. A prophet may also be seen as someone who through divine wisdom speaks as a representative of his or her god and offers wisdom to this world.

Proxy Sitting - Sometimes a séance is arranged where a person agrees to sit in representation of another with the hope of receiving a spirit message on their behalf. This may take place where an individual did not wish to sit with a Spiritualists, whether because nervous or perhaps because of allegiance to another religion that did not consider communication with the spirit world acceptable.

Psi - Abilities which are or appear to be outside of the realms of known science, generally of a paranormal nature.

Psi-Hitting - When a medium achieves a better than average performance when being tested.

Psyche - A word of Greek origin, in simple translation meaning 'soul'.

Psychiatry - Medical terminology for treating people with mental and psychological disorders.

Psychic - An individual who clearly shows psychic ability as in psychometry, pendulum dowsing and other abilities, but who may not necessarily be a medium.

Psychical Research - This is quite old terminology these days, meaning to look at and research the paranormal. You will more often hear of it referred to as parapsychology (see Parapsychology).

Psychic Archaeology - This is where a psychic or medium uses their ability to suggest the best places to find sites of interest for archaeology and artefacts. One of the best-known cases involved Frederick Bligh Bond, who used automatic writing to find and uncover other buildings in and around Glastonbury Abbey in 1907.

Psychic Art - A medium who has the ability to paint or draw, artistically inspired by Spirit.

Psychic Criminology - Many psychics claim that the police force and other such organisations have used their abilities as mediums, and particularly as psychics using psychometry, i.e. by examining and handling people's possessions to find missing people, murdered people, weapons and other efforts to assist the closure of criminal cases. Sir Arthur Conan Doyle stressed on several occasions that eventually the best detectives of the future would be clairvoyants. Many government organisations that do use psychics deny or are reluctant to admit it publicly, but it is a known fact within the Spiritualist movement that on occasions they do.

Psychic Fair - Where a collection of psychics, readers using various predictive methods and stalls selling New Age goods are gathered together and a fee is paid to visit the event.

Psychic Healing - Whereby an individual is given healing from a person using their psychic abilities.

Psychic Lights - See Luminous Phenomena.

Psychic Music - Music that seems to come out of the ether, produced from invisible spirits or entities.

Psychic News - This is the world's oldest and most established newspaper of its kind. The author of this book is a feature columnist in the paper. They can be contacted at Clock Cottage, Stansted Hall, Stansted, Essex, CM24 8UD.

Psychic Phenomena - Unexplained paranormal or

supernormal events or actions.

Psychic Photography - Psychic photos taken using traditional methods: camera, video camera still shot, etc., which feature an extra person present as well as what was seen in the viewfinder, may be considered psychic photography. Much has been made of so-called orbs which are generally refracted light from other light sources such as flashes, etc. Not considered supernormal or spirit photography.

Psychic Rods - Victorian mediums often claimed rods and sticks were formed from ectoplasm in séances and that they could make taps, bangs, even drumming sounds.

Psychic Science - The religion of Spiritualism is a scientific truth which states that at death the inner spirit rises and continues to exist at a higher level.

Psychic Sounds - Unusual unexplained noises.

Psychic Surgery - Some Spiritualist healers claim an ability through spirit guidance to be able to carry out actual operations or perhaps simulate the action on the outside of the body resulting in a procedure happening within the body to remove the cause of the problem. Many psychic surgeons operated in the Philippines and quite a few were considered to be charlatans or masters of sleight of hand techniques, but people have claimed to be helped by psychic surgery. This may need further research and investigation to be totally supported.

Psychic Touches - Many people say that when touched by Spirit it is a sensation similar to the feel of cobwebs across your hands or face.

Psychical Research - Proper scientific examination of all psychic, spiritual, mediumistic and healing claims under controlled test conditions organised by individuals and groups such as the Society for Psychical Research and many others interested in the field.

Psychic World - This is an independent monthly Spiritualist publication which terms itself the independent voice of Spiritualism. The first Psychic World was published in 1946 by founder Maurice Barbanell. It had frequent changes of fortune and success but finally closed down in 1951. The title was brought back into publication in 1993 with intermittent publication until 1994 when it was then taken over by Ray Taylor the former editor of Here and There and Two Worlds and is now published again.

Psychist - A student or other searcher of knowledge of psychology. Sometimes specialising in parapsychology as a subject area.

Psycho-Analysis - To investigate reactions between the sub-conscious and conscious mind with the hope of alleviating psychological problems, or perhaps to treat individuals with mental health conditions. Brought to the wider attention of the world by Dr Sigmund Freud.

Psychogram - A technical term for a message from the other side.

Psycho-Kinesis - Termed PK in the field of parapsychology, whereby experiments are conducted to measure whether something is acting in a paranormal way or at least in a manner not at present recognised by science.

Psychology - The science of understanding consciousness and what makes people react to life and other situations.

Psychometry - First popularised by Dr J. Buchanan in the nineteenth century. He suggested that some individuals could pick up energies or read the history of a certain object by sense and touch. Perhaps more of a psychic ability than mediumistic ability.

Psychoplasm - A rather old word to describe ectoplasm.

Psychosis - A condition of mental illness.

Psychosomatic - When seen as a disorder tends to be better-known today as psycho-physiological illness, whereby symptoms arise that are really caused by mental processes and conditions rather than true physical causes. Where medical diagnosis and examination can find no physical or organic cause then the ailment or condition may be described as psychosomatic (or purely of the mind).

Public Demonstrations - Most Spiritualist churches provide what is known as a divine service on a Sunday which will include a demonstration of mediumship, with the aim of proving to the congregation the truth of life after death. Public demonstrations are sometimes also offered in churches, theatres and large halls where sometimes quite well-known mediums will demonstrate their gift. Those present will pay a fee to watch, as with any other show, but with the promise that for some communication with their loved ones from the other side will be made. Healing is sometimes also demonstrated in churches and at other events but this is not the norm. All such events are under normal lighting conditions, are happy events, and not in any way scary or nerve-wracking.

Purgatory - In the Catholic religion there is a belief that after death some souls for a short period are purged of their sins in a place known as purgatory. Spiritualism does not recognise the existence of such places but puts forward the view that there may be a sphere of love and understanding available for those who have passed under tragic or similar conditions.

Pyramidology - A very old belief structure based around the belief that the height and circumference of the great pyramid in Egypt may relate mathematically to other important sites and historical dates. In more modern times, particularly in the New Age movement, there has been the suggestion that sitting under your own pyramid would bring about balance and wisdom. There is little evidence that this was practised in ancient Egypt and it is not considered important for the development of most Spiritualists.

Qabala - See Cabbala or Kabbala.

Quakers - See Friends, Society of.

Quelle Records - Many considered this to be one of the earliest records relating to the life of Jesus of Nazareth. Originally in Aramaic written format, a Greek translation was considered easier to read and understand. They give a fascinating overview of the life of Jesus but are devoid of the many miracles of the New Testament.

Quinby, Phineas Parkhurst - Came up with the idea of healing known as Mind Cure, which was later developed and presented in a quite similar context by Mary Baker Eddy, who founded the movement known as Christian Science.

Q'umran Members - An ancient Jewish group believed to have been in existence at the end of the second century, close to the area of Wady Q'umran, where many of the Dead Sea scrolls were discovered. On examination of these scrolls some scholars have come to the conclusion that they were the records of the Essenes, of whom Jesus may have been a teacher or Rabbi. The writings suggest a people who practised prayer, healing and were community orientated.

Qu'ran - In simple translation these are the very sacred revelations made by God to Mohammed. For a clearer understanding the author suggests studying the religion of Islam and the book of the Holy Qu'ran in much more detail.

R

Radiesthesia - To dowse with pendulum or dowsing rods. Based around the theory that every living thing gives off some kind of energy or radiation force that is detectable.

Radionics - Use of specialised equipment to measure radiation levels from living things.

Raja-Yoga - The life study and philosophy of yoga.

Randi, James - A professional magician known under the stage name of 'The Amazing Randi', perhaps best-known for his alleged debunking of famous psychics, mediums and other paranormalists. Born in 1928 in Canada, he became a US citizen in 1987. For many years Randi, who lectures all over the world, put up a $1,000,000 prize for the performance of any paranormal occult or supernatural event that could be proved under test conditions. Many psychics and others claim they have met the requirements but as yet have not proven themselves to the satisfaction of Randi and as yet have not received the prize.

Randles, Jenny - Respected researcher of all areas of the paranormal who has written a plethora of books on many areas, such as life after death matters, UFOs, spontaneous human combustion and psychic phenomena. Randles' work is considered serious, analytical and non-judgemental. One of her books that may be of particular interest to Spiritualists is The Afterlife; An Investigation into the Mysteries of Life After Death, although all her books are considered good sources for the investigator of paranormal and psychic research.

Random - A collection of questions are asked of many people to see if there is a common linkage in their answers in the random sample.

Random Events Generator - Specialised equipment which

can electronically select or generate answers, usually numbers.

Random Number Generator - A piece of equipment which used to choose random numbers without prejudice, e.g. the lottery numbers.

Raps - A word often used to describe quiet knocks or taps heard on tables, created through mediumship.

Rapport - A close link between someone or something, such as a medium and their guide.

Rasputin (1865-1916) - Described on different occasions as a Russian mystic, prophet and medium. Claimed to have acted as a psychic for the Russian royal family and made many quite incredible predictions of what was to come for the Romanov Dynasty.

Rationalisation - Where something is said to have a logical explanation.

Raudive Voices - Constantine Raudive is claimed to have discovered the first instances of intelligent voices recorded on magnetic tape. Many people today are interested in the 'white noise' that is heard on radios or the hiss between stations.

Raymond - Was the son of Sir Oliver Lodge. There was also a book written with his name as the title which is of importance in the history of Spiritualism.

Reading - Where information is passed from a medium or psychic to another individual or sitter, they are receiving a reading.

Receptive - A mental attitude which is a requirement for mediumship; a willingness to receive spirit information.

Recurrent Spontaneous Psycho-Kinesis (RSPK) - A term used by parapsychologists for some types of poltergeist activity or attacks.

Regression - Through hypnosis some people believe it is possible to be returned to the early years of their present life and then back into their past lives. Some Spiritualists believe this is a truth, others do not.

Regurgitation - Some mediums, especially in Victorian times, were accused of swallowing material such as cheesecloth and then bringing it back up through the throat and mouth to present as ectoplasm.

Reiki - Pronounced Ray-Key. This is a Japanese word that means universal life energy, an energy that is all around us all the time. Reiki is the name of a way of natural healing which first came into being in Japan through the study and practice of Dr Mikao Usui who died in 1926. During his lifetime he received inspiration to develop and teach others this healing system, which he had brought together through many years of meditative reasoning, study and research. A large part of his life was spent practising Reiki and healing the sick through the techniques he had mastered. He taught others with the instruction that this knowledge must be passed on. Reiki is still taught and passed on to this day by highly trained Reiki masters who have trained and studied extensively, and practised the techniques and traditions that are passed down from master to student. Many Spiritualist mediums and healers, including the author, are also Reiki masters, but there is no specific belief system to be followed in order to learn about Reiki or to receive it, so basically once trained anyone can give or receive treatments.

Reincarnation - The belief that human beings live several lives and return to the earth plane to progress. Some Spiritualists emphatically believe in reincarnation, others totally refute its possibility.

Religion - A belief in God or any faith generally considered of a higher source is considered a religion.

Religion of Spiritualism - Spiritualism is now accepted as a 'proper' religion in Great Britain, many parts of America, and elsewhere in the world. The main belief of Spiritualism is that men and women are spirits and belong to and are part of the Great Spirit. Spiritualism is founded on the belief that there is no death and that mediumship can prove this truth is a vital part of its doctrine.

Remote Viewing (RV) - Some mediums and other sensitives have the ability to see places that are at great distance and sometimes unknown to them, or to see other people in their lives by this method.

Repulsion - The exact reverse of attraction. Working on the theory that like attracts like, a sensitive person may be repulsed or most uncomfortable with an individual that has an aura, or views for that matter, that are most incompatible with their own.

Rescue Circle - In the Spiritualist church some members form what is known as a rescue circle which will specialise in helping spirits that have had difficulty in crossing over, perhaps staying close to the earth plane.

Response - To accept or respond usually in test conditions for a medium or psychic.

Response Bias - Whereby a medium or sensitive tends to react to a particular response or influence.

Resurrection - Probably the most important idea in the Christian church, although some today seem to be of the view that its factuality is not as important perhaps as in the past.

Retro-Cognition - Where a sensitive person claims and has knowledge of past events. (see Déjà Vu).

Revelations - Where without prompt, a medium or other sensitive gives important information, often of global significance.

Reverence - Many religions preach complete reverence and total belief in church elders and ultimately their god. Perhaps not completely in balance with Spiritualism, where interest from all religions is welcome, but there is no insistence on total belief and reverence.

Rhabdomancy - To dowse for water.

Rhine, Professor J. B. - Of Duke University, Ohio, USA. One of the most eminent and respected investigators and researcher of parapsychology, using methods such as Zener Cards, properly testing extra-sensory perception and telepathy, alongside the recognised laws of radiation and physics.

Richet, Dr Charles (1833-1886) - nineteenth century professor of psychology and famous psychic researcher of Paris, France. A leading member of many very important psychical research organisations, he believed hypnotism and hypnotherapy were psychological conditions and not relevant to the magnetic fluids claimed relevant by earlier researchers. A man difficult to tie down to comment, he often said he considered survival unlikely but could not reject its possibility and that a sixth sense may be the answer to many experiences considered paranormal.

Rinaldi, Sonia - Leading researcher of psychical phenomena in the present day.

Ritual Magic - Practices involving ceremonies and rites of a magical nature. Not part of the religion of Spiritualism.

Roberts, Billy - One of the UK's well-known stage psychics, respected medium and author of numerous books. He has appeared on TV and runs his own paranormal study centre in Liverpool. He served Spiritualist churches for many years and now can often be seen working in halls, theatres and at other events.

Roberts, Estelle (1889-1970) - One of the most respected of Spiritualist mediums who displayed a wide variety of abilities including mental mediumship, physical materialisation and direct voice phenomena. Also a very good healer. During the 50s she was very instrumental in getting the Spiritualist religion respected and ultimately legalised in Great Britain, even giving a wonderful demonstration of clairvoyance to the House of Lords, Ladies of the Realm and numerous MPs, who were so impressed that many supported the Spiritualist cause.

Roberts, Ursula - A wonderful Spiritualist medium whose spirit guide was Ramadahn. Many of his words were audio taped then transcribed into book form for those who wished to know wise guidance from the Spirit world, and to gain a greater understanding and better philosophy. Roberts was also an excellent teaching medium who had a reputation of being quite happy to work with all levels of students offering points of advice to the advanced medium, yet even allowing the newest student to address and ask Ramadhan for advice. She was a great worker for Spirit.

Robertson, James - An important early figure in Spiritualism. A Scotsman noted for his straight speaking, authoritative writing and some interesting tests conducted with the great medium, D. D. Home.

Robinson, Derek - The president of Wimbledon Spiritualist church, a fine long-term worker for Spiritualism who has been instrumental in the promotion of many mediums, including Keith Charles. He also runs many courses and offers other opportunities in various areas of Spiritualistic activities. One of the co-founders of LAD Promotions (Life After Death Promotions) alongside Doris Stokes and Gordon Higginson.

Rogers, Rita - Rita Rogers is a medium and psychic who claims to have natural inherent abilities received from her Romany roots. She has written several articles and worked for Bella magazine. She is also the author of several books. Perhaps best-known in the media for reports that suggested she had a close friendship with and worked for Princess Diana.

Roll, Michael - A most interesting writer who propagates the campaign for philosophical freedom and a man whose work will certainly be of great interest to many Spiritualists.

Rosicrucians, The - A society considered very secretive in the fifteenth and sixteenth centuries. It is claimed the society practised healing and academic study but possibly also alchemy and the occult. The society is still around today and may be simply described as looking to develop many faculties within their capabilities. The movement has a symbol which has a rose right in the middle of a cross and some have claimed there may be links between the Rosicrucians and the societies of ancient Egypt.

Roy, Archie - Former president of the Society of Psychical Research, a professor of astronomy, fellow of the Royal Society of Edinburgh, a man of many letters and highly respected authority on all areas of psychical research. The writer of many articles scientifically supported by fine academic research and a man of importance to anyone wishing to source psychic research.

Ruskin, John - A fine English writer and author claimed to have found his belief in the afterlife through the study of Spiritualism.

S

Sabbat - Or Witches Sabbath. Alleged to be a weekly meeting at midnight of witches and warlocks, although probably more of a legendary evernt, most witches being more concerned with healing and helping others than dancing around black candles or calling for Lucifer at the midnight hour. Not considered of interest to true Spiritualists.

Sabbath, The - The Jewish people see the Sabbath or, more appropriately, Shabbat, as a day of rest and reflection, which should be observed from before sundown on Friday until after nightfall on Saturday. The Sabbath for Christian people falls on the Sunday and is again a day of rest when Christians are advised against working or traditionally even taking part in leisure pursuits. In the past shops and most businesses would be closed on the Sabbath. Today there is much more flexibility about what can be done without considering offence to the beliefs of others.

Sabom, Michael - Dr Michael Sabom, MD, a cardiologist who wrote the book Recollections Of Death. Considered of importance in the field of 'near death' research. In 1994 he was instrumental in founding the Atlanta Study, a major investigation of near death experiences (NDEs) with the purpose of looking at life and death experiences that had occurred in hospital theatres on the operating table and other places of death. There are also books published on this area of his work which are important to Spiritualists.

Sacred Writings - Almost all the world's great religions have sacred writings. Spiritualists tend to view all of them as having some wisdom and as a source of inspiration and some Spiritualists may consider the Seven Principles, although fairly modern historically speaking, as their sacred writings.

Sand Reading - Some mystics and indeed some modern day sensitives claim an ability to read a person's character and potential from handprints or footprints in sand.

Sandwich, The Earl of (1839-1916) - Some writings and records suggest the Earl was one of the best early known healers, who once openly said before a medical committee he believed healing could take place. Other records suggest he practiced healing.

Santeria - Spiritualist-type faith from Cuba, though very different to Spiritualism.

Sarjent, Epes - American writer with psychic abilities and credited with bringing the Hydesville case to the public's notice.

Sathya Sai Baba - Probably one of the twentieth century's most talked about gurus. Born in a village, Puttaparthi, in Southern India in 1926, members of his family titled him 'The Little Master'. By the age of five he was known as Brahmanjnani, an incarnation of God. He grew up to perform what thousands described as miracles of healing and other amazing feats. Today he has a massive worldwide following who support him totally. In recent years there have been those who have claimed him to be fraudulent and accused him of very bad things against his followers. Some Spiritualists believe in his work and goodness, others do not.

Satori - A state of enlightenment brought about by meditation.

Saunders, Elsie (1917-1987) - Fine medium and teacher. The mother of Philip Solomon, the author of this book. Former resident of Darlaston Spiritualist church. Awarded the long-service award from the Spiritualists' National Union (SNU).

Saunders, Philip Howard - Born 1925. British medium born Bilston, West Midlands; well-respected medium and teacher.

Savant - From the French for 'knowing'. An academic individual, perhaps a professor or scientist.

Sceptic - People who totally refute anything. Sceptics of Spiritualism would say there is no truth or reality in it at all.

Schiller, Professor - Professor of philosophy of the University of California, USA and man of many letters. In the early 1900s wrote and published 'The progress of psychic research' in the Encyclopaedia Britannica.

Schizophrenia - A mental health condition where conscious and unconscious mind get mixed up. Some have claimed in the past that this condition may be suffered by some mediums. This is a nonsense because trance in mediumship is always under some kind of control at all times and is not allowed when the instrument for Spirit is living their everyday life.

Schneider, Willy Rudi - Tested under very difficult conditions, the brothers always produced good results of paranormal phenomena such as mediumship, levitation, materialisation, etc. Harry Price gave his support to the brothers and vouched for their abilities.

Schwartz, Gary - A professor of psychology, psychiatry, neurology and a highly professional investigator of the afterlife. He has a particularly interesting book for Spiritualists to read and research called The Afterlife Experiments - Breakthrough Scientific Evidence of Life After Death.

Scientology - Teachings and techniques developed and brought to world attention by L. Ron Hubbard, known as Scientology. Also developed from some of his earlier self-help systems, known as Dianetics. A relatively new religion, it is said to offer exact methodology to help humans achieve awareness of their spiritual existence and being through many lifetimes and at the same time become more effective and happy in the physical world

Score - Tally, number or result attained by someone being tested in a psi test.

Scriptography - Words, sentences or messages claimed to have appeared on photographs of the dead, or those still alive, in the perfect hand of people definitely classed as deceased.

Scriptures - The great religions have sacred writings. Those relating to the Bible of the Christian people are called Scriptures. Some Christian Spiritualists find them enlightening, others possibly question their validity on many points.

Scrolls, Dead Sea - See Dead Sea Scrolls.

Scrying - Methods of prediction including looking at items such as a crystal ball, bowls of ink, pools of water, even painted or blackened nails, all fall into the category of scrying.

Seaman, Mrs Judith J. - MSNU. Former president of the

Spiritualist National Union, minister, very good medium and also teacher of other associated subjects. A fine worker for Spiritualism who now resides in Spain.

Séance - From the Victorian times onwards, groups of people would sit together usually round a large table with a medium present in the hopes of communicating with the spirits from the other side.

Séance Room - In the past and sometimes today, some mediums insist on a special room dedicated to demonstrating their work as a medium, which should only be entered by others shortly before a séance is to take place.

Second Sight - An individual who has the ability to sense things of other worlds as a natural gift.

Seer - A person naturally gifted with clairvoyant abilities usually from very early childhood.

Self Control - To exert one's own will on yourself to control various behaviour, actions or thoughts. Relevant to the boundaries every individual sets themselves in their life. Considered an important consideration in the work of any medium.

Sensing - Mediums often speak of sensing Spirit, describing it as being close by. A psychometrist uses sensing to describe what they get from objects they touch and feel.

Sensitive - Another name for a psychic or someone with mediumistic ability.

Sepulchre - Funeral tomb, as in the Holy Sepulchre that held the body of Jesus Christ. Important to Christian Spiritualists.

Seraph - Angels of the highest order, always claimed to be praising God.

Serialism - Descriptive word used by J. W. Dunne after his research into precognition in the dream state and his theory of time and cause. Some Spiritualists believe that some dreams have meaning or can come true.

Service - A service in Spiritualism is where a medium speaks from the platform or rostrum assisted by a chairperson who supports and leads the service. Sometimes a reading is given from the speaker and in some but not all, hymns are sung. The medium then gives a demonstration of mediumship to prove the existence of life ever after. Service is sometimes spoken of in Spiritualism in terms of anyone who dedicates their life to church work or the wider advancement of the truth of Spiritualism.

Seven Principles - In Spiritualism there is no real fixed creed but there are seven principles that are in use and advised by the Spiritualist National Union, with the suggestion that all may interpret each and every one in their own way. They are
1) The Fatherhood of God, 2) The Brotherhood of Man, 3) The Communion of Spirits and the Ministry of Angels, 4) The Continuous existence of the human soul, 5) Personal responsibility, 6) Compensation and retribution hereafter for all the good and evil deeds done here on Earth, 7) Eternal progress open to every soul.

Shakers - Early American religious group aligned to the Quakers and others. The name shakers is said to be relevant to the slight shaking of an individual before inspired speech. This has occurred to some mediums before they have worked too.

Shaman - The priests of some tribes, perhaps a medicine man or woman, a witch doctor, or others with spiritual understanding and knowledge.

Shape-Shifting - Supernormal ability to take on or assume the form of another human being, creature or entity.

Shine, Betty (1929-2002) - Spiritual healer, medium, writer and author of many fine books of a spiritual nature. Some of her best works of particular interest to Spiritualists today are found in the Mind Series, which includes the books Mind To Mind, Mind Waves, and My Life as a Medium, amongst others.

Siddhi - Great physical power believed to be obtainable by some highly developed practitioners of yoga and other Eastern traditions.

Sign - Many mediums and sensitives believe they are given signs, such as lights over people in congregations and audiences, to suggest a link is being made between them, the medium and the spirit world.

Silence - Many Spiritualists believe a short period of silence before any work brings you into better preparation for attunement with the spirit world.

Silver Birch - One of the most loved of guides and the native American control and guide of Maurice Barbanell. Also came through in Hannen Swaffer's circle. A guide of most beautiful wisdom that is as relevant today as it would have been throughout time. Silver Birch has many admirers in Spiritualism and many books have been written with his inspiration. Some of the best have been put together and edited by Tony Ortzen, the former editor of Psychic News.

Silver Cord - This is the link said to exist between the physical and astral body, which separates at death (see Astral Cord).

Simultaneous Dreams - When two people or more have the same dream at the same time.

Sin - Many religious organisations speak of sin, the first one being between Adam and Eve. Some religions believe that through confession, sins can be forgiven. Spiritualists tend to take the view that all wrong done must be put right in this world.

Sitter - An individual that has a reading with a medium on a one-to-one basis is often described as a sitter.

Sitting - In the past sometimes a séance was described as a group sitting.

Sixth Sense - A word used many times to describe many experiences, a sort of ability that all have but not everyone knows how to tune into.

Slate Writing - Unexplainable writing produced on slates, generally in the past as part of a séance. Tends to be the work of conjurers, magicians and generally fraudulent mediums and psychics.

Sleep Paralysis - A condition that can be quite alarming. When someone is quite conscious and awake but cannot move a muscle.

Sleep State - The nocturnal experience of closing your eyes and going to sleep to dream and to rest.

Smells, Psychic - Aromas have always been associated with spirit entities often with the perfume of a person giving a clue to their being around, so to speak. A fragrance of flowers, particularly lavender, is also a common smell picked up by sensitives and others.

Smith, Gordon - Well-known practising British medium of

Glasgow, Scotland. Described as the psychic barber, Gordon spent much of his life balancing his work as a demonstrating medium alongside his hairdressing career. His very popular demonstrations have gained him the reputation of being a very good medium both at home and abroad. He appeared on a BBC 'Everyman' documentary called 'Talking with the Dead' and is the author of two successful books. He also has popular columns for magazines and newspapers and for a short time acted as the medium on 'Most Haunted', the TV programme presented by Yvette Fielding.

Smith, Suzie - Used to run the Survival Research Foundation in America and is the writer of a plethora of books, emphasising her belief in and research of the possibility of communication with spiritual worlds.

Solar Plexus - Situated in the lower area of the stomach, many mediums and other sensitives believe that stimulation of this area assists with their ability to link with Spirit and to bring themselves into perfect balance. This is sometimes achieved through breathing techniques. Acclaimed former editor of Psychic News, Maurice Barbanell, told of hearing disincarnate voices speaking from this area of some mediums' bodies.

Somnambule - Describes the very deep hypnotic condition. Also descriptive of a person doing something physically whilst still asleep, such as sleepwalking.

Sorcery - To cast evil spells as part of Black Magic practice. Never a part of Spiritualism.

Soul - A word that some people describe as the higher self. It is applicable for Spiritualists to speak of this as Spirit, for they know that at death the spirit or soul continues to operate in the etheric spirit world. The higher part of an individual that Christians and others describe as immortal.

Soul, Old - (See Old Soul).

Southcott, Joanna (or Southcote) (1750-1814) - Claimed that in 1792 the Spirit of Truth told her much information about the Earth's future. Her spirit guide told her that some of the information that he gave her must be sealed in a large box which could only in the future, at a time of great threat to the world, be opened by 24 bishops of the Church of England. The box is still said to be in existence and held by the Panacea Society. Some claim it still has an important part to play for the world to this day. Joanna Southcott's story of spirit communication and her box is still be a very interesting story to read and research today.

Space Time - Some people have hypothesised the view that the universe has a four-dimensional state of depth, breadth, length and time.

Speaking in Tongues - For someone in trance to speak with a voice in a language and dialect not known to them or anyone else.

Spear of Destiny - Sometimes called the sacred spear or lance of the Roman soldier Longinus which was used to pierce the side of Jesus whilst on the cross. Claimed by some nations to still exist and to have the ability to make them undefeatable in battle. Some stories maintain that the true spear was in possession of the Nazis during the Second World War.

SPE - Subjective Paranormal Experiences.

Spectre - Simply put, an apparition.

Speculum - Something that refracts light that shines upon it and can be looked at meditatively for inner wisdom. Mystics probably use a crystal ball at times for this practices, due to its obvious ability to draw light.

Specularii - The name given to those that practised scrying in the 1500s.

Spell - Spoken or written words with the intent to harm, control, or in White Magic practices sometimes to help heal and change situations for the better.

Spheres - Many believe there are several spheres or levels of spirit life. Some mediums such as the author, believe there are seven.

Spheres, Celestial - The planets some Spiritualists believe may have intelligent life upon them. Others Spiritualists do not believe this.

Spirit - This word is often used to describe any discarnate body. Any entity may also be described as spirit but generally when Spiritualists speak of Spirit, they are describing loved ones that have gone before and others that have progressed to a higher level of wisdom and understanding, yet still wish to help us in this world.

Spirit Children - Spiritualists do not believe that birth takes place in the spirit world but any child that dies in the physical womb for whatever reason or before growing up in our world continues to develop, grow and progress, generally under the guidance and love of family members and others in the spirit world. Spirit children have often been known to work with mediums as their guides, come back to the this world and be the secret friends or playmates of physical children, and are always special spirits much loved by those in this and the other world and never without love and family around them.

Spirit Communications - (See Communication).

Spirit Councils - Some communication from Spirit suggests that some spirits gather in groups to discuss their ideas as to how best they can progress themselves and those in our world.

Spirit Cure - When healing takes place that is believed to result from help, direct or indirect, from a spirit being.

Spirit Doctors - It is not surprising that many physicians, highly skilled surgeons and doctors when they pass to the other side try to find mediums who they can work through in our world to continue to help those that are sick.

Spirit, Great - This is the way many Spiritualists describe the mother god figure and spirit itself collectively and individually.

Spirit Guide - A spirit from the other side who looks after and assists a medium in this world, often called a control in the past.

Spirit Healing - (See Healing).

Spirit Helper - (See Helper).

Spiritism - A word or philosophy that became quite popular in nineteenth-century France. There are many similarities to Spiritualism, but many who follow this particular pathway believe and teach that reincarnation exists too, whereas many in British Spiritualism do not consider it a reality (see Spiritualism).

Spirit Lights - Many mediums and sensitives see Spirit as gold and silver orbs or collectively in flashes of beautiful coloured lights.

Spirit Operation - Some mediums claim they have the ability to perform operations inspired through a guide or control who was either a physician or surgeon in their lifetime. In the

Philippines many psychic surgeons do this work but many are considered fraudulent.

Spirit Photography - Photographs of spirits, sometimes quite solid, others quite spectral, such as mists or collections of orbs, spheres, etc.

Spirit Spheres - (See Spheres).

Spirit Teacher - A spirit who wishes to influence and teach individuals in this group wisdom, inspiration and sometimes the correct philosophy for the religion of Spiritualism.

Spiritualism - Is a science, religion, philosophy and way of life, grounded in the truth that there is no death. It differs from many religions in that during its services there is generally a medium who gives a demonstration to prove this fact with messages from the spirit world, which can be clearly recognised and accepted by members of the congregation or others present.

Spiritualist - A person who has come to accept as fact that truths and evidence given through mediumship from those in the spirit world to those in our world prove emphatically that life continues after death. They also believe that there is a hierarchy of progression for spirit people that is available to us that ultimately leads to a unified consciousness of all with God, the Great Spirit. Many Spiritualists are part of and members of the Spiritualists' National Union (SNU) some are Christian Spiritualists. All Spiritualists believe death is not the end and all spirits including those in this world are a part of working towards ultimate combined consciousness and God.

Spiritualist Association of Great Britain - Founded in London, England, in 1872, to study psychic phenomena. Today it is one of the most respected organisations in the Spiritualist movement, provides some very good mediums for people to consult, as well as healers, with membership open to everyone regardless of their faith or religion. Its headquarters is also a lovely building to visit at 33 Belgrave Square, London.

Spiritualists' National Union (SNU) - The largest Spiritualist organisation in Europe, brought into being in 1890 to propagate the religion of Spiritualism, structured around its seven principles. Has the aim of bringing all Spiritualist churches eventually under its leadership. Provides training opportunities with certificates and diplomas for mediums, healers and others to work towards. Also encompasses the Lyceum movement, which educates and makes young people aware of Spiritualism and its life pathways. It is based at Redwoods, Stansted Hall, Stansted, Essex, CM24 8UD.

Spirit World - A word to describe the plane where spirit people continue their existence in the higher life.

Spontaneous Experiences - When paranormal phenomena happens quite unexpectedly in everyday life.

Spontaneous Human Combustion - Where someone or something suddenly catches fire without any obvious cause. Several bodies have been found, often the bottom part of the torso, half to three-quarters burned away with no obvious cause, though some experts have hypothesised the view they may have burned rather like a candle.

SPR, The - The Society for Psychical Research.

Square - In astrology an angle of 90 degrees between the positions of two planets.

Statistics - A form of maths used to analyse, interpret and predict possibilities. A good way to measure mediums' and psychics' ability under test conditions.

St Paul - The story of the Epistle of St Paul is of great relevance to many Spiritualists who claim it may be the first-known written and recorded example in the modern world that shows clearly those in the spirit or higher world advising and communicating with someone in this world. The enlightenment claimed to have been given to St Paul on the road to Damascus can be seen as an example of this. The modern Spiritualist healer, Ray Browne, claims St Paul works through him to heal today and was the subject of a TV documentary.

Steiner, Rudolf (1861-1925) - The original founder of Anthroposophy. Born in Austria with good clairvoyant abilities, he is also credited with bringing his views into specialised education, which has been claimed to especially benefit autistic and other young people with learning difficulties. There are many Rudolf Steiner schools throughout Britain today.

Stevenson, Robert Louis - Famous author who many claimed was greatly interested and helped by Spiritualism through his friendship with D. D. Home, whom he linked his friends with, to conduct psychic experiments. At one time held a high position in the Scottish Spiritualist association.

Sthenometer - A piece of equipment invented by Dr Paul Joire to measure energies and forces he felt were given out by a medium's physical body and aura. Could be collected in metal, wood and water in much the same way electricity can be.

Stigmata - Some people claim and show physical marks or wounds passing through their hands and feet that suggest they have been punctured paranormally by nails to recreate the injuries suffered by Jesus Christ at his crucifixion. This seems to be as popular in some countries today as it has ever been.

Stimulus - Some mediums and psychics claim they work better when everything is very quiet, such as trance mediumship, and with little light. Some also claim equipment such as a red light is a useful stimulus to bring forth or attract spirits.

Stockwell, Tony - Practising medium, Tony was born in the East End of London, England. He has spent the last few years demonstrating mediumship all over the world. He also teaches and lectures at the College of Psychic Studies in London. Likewise, sometimes at the Arthur Findlay College, Stansted Hall. He had a successful television series called the 'Street Psychic' where he would stop people on the street and give them readings, and also the 'Psychic Detective', where he investigated crimes of the past. A close friend of Colin Fry, they sometimes demonstrate in theatres together. He also writes on occasions in the Psychic News. In 1999 he was a co-founder of the Avalon Project to promote and encourage spiritual learning, development and understanding.

Stokes, Doris - Undoubtedly Britain's best-known and probably best-loved medium. Doris Stokes was considered to be one of the most evidentially accurate mediums there has ever been. Travelling all over the world and appearing at many major theatres, including the Sydney Opera House and the London Palladium, Doris was the one medium who could always be guaranteed to put the 'House Sold Out' signs up. It is probable that Doris was a clairaudient medium who mostly heard spirit voices, but incredibly relayed the messages they had for people in this world once she felt or saw who the message was for. Doris Stokes had many stories written about her and also had numerous best-selling books. Perhaps the best way you could describe her was that she was a sort of 'everyone's grandma' figure. Many television and media appearances were given across the world before her passing to the spirit world on the 8th May, 1987. Many other media mediums have tried to replace Doris but in truth no-one has really succeeded as yet.

Stone Throwing - Many examples of small stones either coming from unseen hands or sometimes raining down on roofs have been recorded throughout history.

Subconscious Cooperation - Trance mediumship requires that the medium in varying states and degrees gives over his or her consciousness to a control or spirit from the other side, confidently protected by their own guide.

Subconscious Mind - This is the part of the mind of which we are not immediately aware and needs some sort of stimulus to bring to the front of our thinking.

Subjective Paranormal Experience (SPE) - Whereby an experience singularly or collectively, such as in a group, is considered to be paranormal by the majority.

Subliminal - A word from the fields of psychology describing the mental awareness level that is beneath normal conscious-ness. Can also be considered as pleasurable in context.

Sufism - An important part of the religion of Islam which has eight holy rules and principles. The author suggests further study of the Islamic faith for a better understanding.

Suggestion - All mediums and sensitives have to be careful not to pick up on anything that might be seen as suggestion from this world rather than influence from the spirit world.

Summerland - A description of the Spirit World coined by H. A. Davis. Some Spiritualists believe that the spirit world can be anything an individual wishes it to be when they go there and that all of the pleasures of this world, such as animals, the seaside, loved ones, home conditions, etc. will be there as you would wish it to be.

Superconscious Mind - A description used by F. W. H. Myers to describe the higher understanding and use of one's conscious mind as a tool for sensitivity and intuition.

Supernatural - Any example of phenomena which cannot be answered by science or by natural laws. Spiritualists would suggest and do believe that mediumship, for example, is not supernatural, but rather falls within scientific laws that can be investigated, discovered and proven.

Supreme Spirit - Terminology sometimes used by Spiritualists to describe the complete unified consciousness all are progressing towards, or in more simple terminology, God.

Surgery, Spirit - Some healers today claim the ability to be able to operate on people and give psychic or spirit surgery. It is something that Spirit is capable of achieving through a medium healer in this world but has been dogged by fraudulent practitioners.

Survey - To collect opinions or data usually by interview or questionnaire. Sometimes used at large Spiritualist gatherings to gain a random sample of the general opinion of the ability of the mediums, healers, psychics and sensitives present. Newspapers and magazines often conduct such surveys.

Survival - The whole basis of Spiritualism revolves around the truth of survival, that is, there is no death.

Swaffer, Hannen (1879-1962) - Professional journalist and accomplished speaker, who conducted many closed circle experiments with many fine mediums. Eventually took over as president of the SNU after Sir Arthur Conan Doyle. One of the great champions for Spiritualism who certainly helped to bring a professional voice from the religion to the mass media. He also appeared in several films including Death at Broadcasting House, Late Extra and Spellbound. A committed socialist, he left the Labour Party in 1957 and is claimed to have written a million words each year. A truly great Spiritualist of modern times.

Swedenborg, Emanuel (1688-1772) - Founder member of the society of Swedenborgianism. Not only a fine very early days medium, but scientist, astronomer, zoologist, and extensive writer about psychic experiences and development which can certainly be aligned to and compared with Spiritualism as we know it today. He would have been a strong theological thinking man, yet in many ways could be titled the first Spiritualist, who clearly put forward the view that there was no such thing as death and that another world was there for all that would be very much like the one they currently, existed in, except etherical rather than physical.

Sylph - Small Spirit entities considered part of the elements of air; semi-transparent, winged flying creatures probably very similar, if not the same, as fairies.

Symbolism - An example of symbolism would be a person seeing a cloud when scrying or looking at a crystal ball, perhaps suggesting rainy days are coming.

Synchronicity - Carl Jung termed synchronicity as coincidences that had measured meaning, but not generally with a common cause that could be easily identified. (Read Jung's work in this field for a more detailed explanation).

T

Table Tilting - Movement of a table often took place in séances of yesteryear where several people, with their fingertips lightly placed on a table, believed Spirit would tilt or move the furniture without their assistance in any way (see Table Turning).

Table Turning - Perhaps three people place their fingers on the top of a table, then start to rock the table backwards and forwards. People then move, lift or turn the table round with no obvious physical assistance from the people present. Some claim this is simply a rather clever trick, others that it is the result of telekinesis and that it is mediumistic ability in one or all the people present which is responsible for table turning examples.

Tao - Meaning the absolute, or way of nature. The Taoist way accepts passively what will be.

Tãpãs - A practice or exercise from the field of yoga claimed to help free or lift the spirit from the physical body.

Target - Some mediums and psychics under test conditions have moved objects a measurable distance, sometimes under glass domes called targets.

Tarot - A very old method of divination that influences sensitives to give advice to others from strong symbolic pictures on the cards. A proper tarot pack always has 78 cards split into two arcanas which consist of the minor arcane with 56 cards, and the major arcane with 22 cards. Considered an important tool for those of the Romany traditions, probably natural sensitives, and highly popular with those of the New Age movement, some of whom have invented or designed their own packs which in many ways are very different to the original tarot and probably used more in a supportive role to their claimed sensitive gifts.

Teachers - Anyone who has wisdom especially spiritually might be described as a teacher. There are those in the Spiritualist movement today who specifically take on the role of developing others mediumistically in healing skills and in the philosophy of the religion.

Telekinesis - This is where objects are moved at the will of an individual who has no physical connection with them, but simply uses the power of the mind.

Telepathy - The ability to read another person's thoughts, pick up their feelings, etc. through paranormal ability. Telepathy would be considered more a psychic ability than the similar work of clairvoyants, for example, who would be receiving the information from a third party, i.e. spirit being.

Teleportation - Whereby objects by supernormal effort are sent elsewhere, usually dematerialising and then reappearing somewhere else.

Telescope Vision - Some sensitives describe an ability to see things more clearly through bringing themselves into a way of viewing as if through a telescope. It is also claimed by some that they use this method for remote viewing - the ability to see something that is happening many miles from where they are. This is probably a psychological prop to assist the medium to believe in his or her abilities.

Temporal - Relevant to earthly life and things that can be measured by time and space.

Temporal Lobe Activity - When stimulation occurs in the temporal lobe part of the brain, some individuals are said to have unusual experiences which might cause hallucinations, or unexplainable visions. Some psychiatrist think this may be the answer to the visions of the clairvoyant.

Testimony - To speak truthfully or make a statement of definite fact.

Thaumaturgy - When a miracle happens through superhuman help, for example where the eight stone mother lifts a car that has trapped her child and neither she or anyone else knows where the strength came from.

Theosophy - Madame Blavatsky was founder member of the Theosophical Society. She called it wisdom religion and felt that it would be a new starting point for all the world's great philosophies and religions. It includes reincarnation and the development of psychic abilities for all its members.

Therianthropy - The alleged capability of some human beings to turn into animal beings and then back into human form.

Theurgy - A word that describes an intention or effort to communicate with ascended beings or gods.

Third Eye - This is an invisible eye that mediums and psychics talk about as being positioned just above the two normal eyes. Considered by many to be where all psychic work is done. Some mediums say that with their eyes closed they clearly see Spirit with the third eye.

Thought Forms - These are apparitions that are said to build up from the thoughts of those of a sensitive or mediumistic nature capable of projecting energy in this way.

Thought Photography - Many experiments have taken place on thought photography whereby tests have been carried out on individuals who have been able to will images onto film still inside cameras or onto photographs that have already been taken.

Thought Power - The power of thought is considered important, especially by clairaudient mediums, who say they can pick up thought power influences from the spirit world that have positive meaning to those in this world. Some also claim that by thoughts they can cause change and action to physically happen to objects and sometimes other people.

Thought Transference - The communication of minds, as in telepathy.

Time - Many mediums claim they have received information from their guides, controls and other spirits that time is different in the spirit world to that which is known to us in this world. This may be the reason why it takes some spirits recently passed over longer to come through and let their loved ones know of their safe passing over. Indeed sometimes years may pass before a message is received.

Tongues, Talking in - See Xenoglossy.

Torah - Ancient Jewish law, sometimes called the Pentateuch. Many laws were claimed to be taught by Moses to the Israelites after speaking with God in a mediumistic sort of way.

Trance - The trance that mediums speak of is a little like sleep conditions whereby the physical body may still have some activity, but the conscious mind gives up varying levels of control to disincarnate bodies and spirits.

Trance Medium - An individual who goes into varying levels of trance before allowing spirit influence to exemplify the existence of Spirit by producing their words and sometimes actions for others.

Transcendental Meditation - Maharishi Mahesh, yogi, brought to the Western world the teachings and techniques of transcendental meditation. Many 60s pop stars and other celebrities learned this technique and life pathway.

Transcendental Music - This is where music from an unexplained non-physical source can clearly be heard. In more modern times and particularly as part of the New Age movement transcendental music tends to be beautiful, relaxing music probably played from a CD or MP3 player.

Transfiguration - This is physical mediumship which should result in the medium's face changing to what is a very good likeness of a person now in Spirit, usually in the form of a mask over the medium's face made from ectoplasm. Some mediums insist on darkened conditions, but a few have performed transfiguration in ordinary daylight.

Transmigration of Souls - This is the belief in the rebirth of souls or spirits in any form, animal or human.

Transportation - This is the claimed ability that some human beings can pass through walls, space, perhaps even to another country through supernormal intentions to do so. Some mediums and psychics have reportedly achieved this whilst witnessed by others, for example the Davenport Brothers, the Pansini Brothers, who claimed to be witnessed by an official officer of the pope, and in more recent times, famous paranormalist Uri Geller.

Transposition of the Senses - Some mediums during trance states have drawn close to the aromas, tastes, smells and other senses, which can also be experienced by those present.

Tree of Life - Symbolises the unity of everything in the universe and its links and interactions. An important part of Kabbala, it is suggested further reading is undertaken to understand the importance of the Tree of Life, to some Spiritualists.

Trevelyan, Sir George - Fourth Baronet, who was very proud of his ancestry, which may have linked him to King Arthur's knights and also to Lyonesse, the legendary island that sank off the coast of Cornwall. Educated at Cambridge University, Sir George had several academic teaching posts. He also had a great attraction towards the mystical and presented a course entitled 'Death and Becoming', which at that time would have been difficult for him to present amongst his peers. He was also very involved in the foundation of the Findhorn Foundation and considered by many to be one of the father figures of the coming New Age movement. Some of his books are quite outstanding and should be of interest to Spiritualists and others. One in particular, amongst many, A Vision of the Aquarian Age, may be of interest. In 1971, Sir George also set up the Wrekin Trust to promote spiritual education and knowledge.

Trine - An angle of 120 degrees between two planets generally thought of as beneficial in a horoscope in the field of astrology.

Trumpet - In the past trumpets made of metal or sometimes just cardboard were used to direct voice phenomena by many Victorian mediums and to a lesser extent more recently. They were sometimes placed at the mouth of the medium or at other times floated about the room. Jonathan Koons was a well-known early American medium who brought this to great popularity in the séance rooms of America. It is little-used today when we have microphones and amplifiers to project the quieter direct voice phenomena.

Tumbler and Letters - An oft-used quick way of assembling a home-made Ouija board was to place an upturned tumbler or glass in front of or round a circle of letters. Individuals would then place a finger on the tumbler which it is claimed would slide towards the letters and numbers to spell out names, etc. Spiritualism does not recommend such foolish party games which can have inherent dangers (See Ouija Board).

Twain, Mark (1835-1910) - Highly acclaimed American author. Also had belief in psychic phenomena and paranormal investigation. Twain is claimed to have returned with evidence from the other side to several mediums over the years.

Tweedale, Violet - Born around 1862. Fine writer and composer of important early books on Spiritualism. Claimed to have attended and organised séances with James Balfour, Gladstone, and Lord Haldane, helping to bring respect and academic interest to the early days of Spiritualism.

Twigg, Ena (1914-1969) - Fine medium and teacher. The first Spiritualist minister to be featured on a mainstream religious programme for BBC television in the 1960s. In some of her private sittings was said to have given survival evidence to kings and queens, politicians and the rich and famous, but said to have been just as caring to ordinary everyday people with messages to prove their loved ones continued on the other side. She became very well known, not just in her native England, but in America and many European countries too and was considered a fine worker in many ways for Spiritualism.

Twin Soul - More often today the words 'soulmate' is used to describe spirits that incarnate time after time together in many lifetimes.

Two Worlds - Excellent magazine edited by Tony Ortzen. Can be contacted at 7 The Leather Market, Weston Street, London, SE1 3ER.

Typtology - See Table Turning.

Ufology - Many people today study UFOs and form groups to watch for them in specific areas of the world where regular occurrences of such craft are claimed to be seen. Ufology itself might be best thought of as the more scientific way of examining them.

Ultra-Perceptive Faculty - The ability to read and pick up information from someone or something by sight, hearing and touch. Psychometrists believe there is a sort of psychic record that stays with objects such as jewellery and even clothes.

Umbanda - A Spiritist faith that has its grounding in Brazil. Not really similar to true Spiritualism with some aspects perhaps being part of the voodoo religion.

Undine - Element spirits associated with water. Best described as tiny creatures with wings that are shaped rather like fins.

Unfoldment - A word describing development in areas such as mediumship, healing and other philosophy of Spiritualism.

Unidentified Flying Object (UFO) - Any unexplained objects, lights, and other items that are projected in the sky could be described as UFOs. Many people have seen objects flying in the sky that are claimed not to be of this world, including the author, famous personalities of show business, sport and even a president. Some Spiritualists think this may suggest extra-terrestrial life on other planets and that some of these crafts may have such beings or entities on board. Other Spiritualists do not consider this to be likely.

Unitarian - A member of a religious group which claims the unity of divine nature, rather than the acceptance of the Trinity in Christianity, for example.

Universalism - The idea that in the end all of us will be brought to spiritual and physical fulfilment or in the more associated Christian term 'saved'.

Universal Mind - Words first used by J. A. Findley to describe the higher mind substance gained through attunement to the spirit vibration. He described it as the all-encompassing creative power of the universe.

Vale-Owen, Reverend George (1869-1931) - Traditional English vicar who experimented with and developed the art of automatic writing. Yet it was not until after his death that his work was extensively publicised. During his lifetime he had been offered large amounts of money to have his work examined but always refused. During the latter part of his life, he became a minister of a Spiritualist group and travelled to many parts of America and also wrote important books describing the truth of the afterlife and the existence of the spirit world.

Valiantine, George - American direct voice medium whose supporters claimed through his mediumship the return of Confucius and an ongoing commentary on ancient Chinese literature and history. One of the first mediums to have his work recorded on a gramophone record in 1927.

Vampire - The legend of the vampire is of a spirit that will not join the spirit world but has taken possession of a living entity or body to carry on enjoying the physical pleasures of the living world. Vampires have become quite famous through various films suggesting a creature that will bite and draw blood from its victim, Bram Stoker's Dracula being the perfect example. Many consider this purely legend but it is a fact that in some parts of Europe, especially in the country areas, some people of farming stock still put up rings of garlic on doors and windows to protect them from evil spirits.

Vandermeulen Spirit Indicator - A sort of doorbell piece of equipment with a line between the medium and a press connection covered by glass. This would be claimed to be rung by the spirit upon imminent communication being likely.

Van Praagh, James - James was born in Bayside, New York, the youngest of four children. Raised a Catholic and altar boy. Entering the seminary at the age of 14 it is claimed this is where his interest in Catholicism ended and his interest in spirituality and mediumship first started. Van Praagh also obtained a degree from San Francisco State University in Broadcasting but at 24 his main involvement in life was metaphysics and psychic phenomena. He started doing psychic readings for friends and quickly found himself becoming a demonstrating medium and eventually made several appearances on the MBC talk show 'The Other Side', and became extremely popular appearing on 'Oprah', 'Larry King Live', 'Maury Povich', '20-20' and '48 Hours', making him a psychic superstar in America and other parts of the world. He eventually hosted his own shows, namely 'Beyond with James Van Praagh', 'Living with the Dead', 'Ghost Whisperer' and others. His books, CDs, seminars and classes are all highly popular with an international fan base.

Vanishing Objects - Some mediums, mystics, sensitives and others claim the ability to make things dematerialise and go to other places (see Apports).

Vates - The spirit guide of the Reverend Stainton Moses who some believed may have been the Biblical Daniel.

Veda - An ancient religion or part of the Hindu faith followed by many members of the Asian community.

Vedanta - Hindu truths based upon the Vedas.

Vegan - A vegetarian who will not eat any meat or anything that includes animal by-products. Some Spiritualists today are Vegans, others are not.

Vegetarian - A person who will not eat meat believing that in some cases animals are also progressing spirit entities on an evolutionary progression in the same way as men and women. Many Spiritualists today are vegetarians because they are opposed to the slaughter of animals.

Ventriloquism - Some parapsychologists and investigators of paranormal activity have suggested that some fraudulent psychics have used ventriloquism (the ability to speak without moving the lips) to present examples of direct voice mediumship and other audial psychic phenomena.

Veridical - An experience or event that can be positively verified by perhaps several sources, photographic evidence or expert opinion.

Veridical Dream - When you have a dream that in the waking state can be checked out and verified to be factual, usually in a past or past-tense context.

Vibrations - You will often hear Spiritualists speak of vibrations. In simple terms this is the mental attunement between the two worlds. Some mediums, the author included, believe everything vibrates and you must quicken your vibration to work spiritually and slow it a little to work psychically.

Vishnu - The divine one or spokesman on Earth for the Bhagavadgita. Some Hindus and others claim throughout history that there have been individuals being incarnated as Vishnu to speak of and teach the sacred knowledge.

Vision - To see physical objects and matter with your physical eyes.

Vision, Clairvoyance - See Clairvoyance.

Vision, Spontaneous - See Apparitions and Spectres.

Vision, Telescopic - See Telescopic Vision.

Visionary - A person considered of great wisdom and knowledge before their time. Many Spiritualist pioneers were described as visionaries.

Visitants - The appearance of a spirit person or a ghost.

Visualisation - Spiritualist mediums will often use the term visualisation to describe the creation of something in the mind's eye of a physical context, i.e. visualising energy around all things.

Vital Body - Words that describe the etheric body.

Voice Box - This is the apparatus that is created by Spirit from ectoplasm etherically within the medium to produce the sound of the human voice, in the likeness of disincarnate voices.

Voice Control Machines - Many machines have been invented to test whether direct voice phenomena is independent of any other medium's conscious influences. In the past they were considered very inaccurate. Today with the advancement of electronics, some equipment is producing good results but further tests are required to prove their accuracy.

Voice, The - Words used in Spiritualism to speak of the direct voice phenomena that emanates from the medium.

Voices, Independent - This is where voices are heard from sources detached from the working medium, though sometimes it can be heard from other present materialised forms.

Voodoo - This is a spirit-generated religion that also includes aspects of ancestor worship, a unique type of trance mediumship and which often involves the sacrifice of animals, ritual dances and secret wisdom. It has an ancient existence in places such as Haiti, the West Indies and some parts of America, probably taken there originally by slaves, and has aspects that are still practised in parts of Africa. Many other religions are also said to be taken and incorporated into its modern practices, such as Catholicism and Spiritualism, but both these religions would probably distance themselves from many of its practices.

Vortex - A whirlpool or whirlwind of paranormal context considered by some to be a link between the two worlds.

Walker, Nea - Sir Oliver Lodge's personal secretary in matters regarding psychic and paranormal research and a well-respected researcher of psychical matters in her own right.

Wallace, Dr Alfred Russell (1832-1903) - Naturalist and claimed co-discover, of Charles Darwin's principles of evolution, who later developed an interest in Spiritualism, leading to him working with and testing famous mediums of the time, such as Katie Cook.

Walpurgis Night - On the eve of the 1st May, German legend holds that witches meet with evil spirits and the Devil himself annually on this night.

Walter - The guide and control of Margery Crandon. In some communications Walter claimed to be Margery's brother who had passed tragically some years before.

Warlock - This is a male witch (see Witch).

Water Divining - See Dowsing.

Water, Perfume - A phenomenon that happened fairly regularly in the early days of Spiritualism and séances. Those present would experience droplets of perfumed water falling on them from the air often with fragrances such as lavender, lilies and roses.

Watson, Lyall - Born 1930. Zoologist, botanist, biologist, anthropologist, ethnologist. Also the writer of numerous New Age books, perhaps the one of most interest to Spiritualists being Supernature. In this highly acclaimed book he tries to increase understanding between natural and what is considered supernatural phenomena in biological expression. One time director of the Johannesburg Zoo, South Africa and former producer and writer for BBC documentaries, Watson spends much of his life today in Ireland.

Webber, Jack - Fine British physical medium born in Wales. Received great acclaim for the ability to produce apports (gifts from the spirit world for others). Excellent direct voice medium, claimed to be able to levitate. Webber developed in the healer Harry Edwards' home circle. Many modern Spiritualists today are very interested in the words of Jack Webber.

Wells, David - Born in Scotland before joining the Royal Navy, followed by a career in catering, he found himself becoming interested in the psychic world. He eventually developed a career as an astrologer and studied other psychic arts, before becoming resident medium on the 'Most Haunted' television series presented by Yvette Fielding.

Werewolf - An ancient tradition within supernormal claims, or perhaps more appropriately legends, claims that some human beings could, under certain stimuli, be turned into wolves or half-man, half-wolf-type creatures (see Shape-Shifting).

Wheel of Life - This is often seen on cards or drawings. The wheel represents life as forever turning, starting, progressing and ending, then starting all over again.

White Brotherhood, The Great - Many people from the New Age movement brought this term back into popular use. In simple terminology it suggests there is a group of masters or ascended entities, spirits, etc., guiding the universe and our world.

White, Stuart Edward (1873-1946) - American who studied at the University of Michigan. Wrote several books on information channelled from the other side. The Unobstructed Universe came out in 1940 and is still considered an important overview of his metaphysical work.

White Magic - Some practitioners of Wiccan ways or white witchcraft perform healing, including spells for the good of themselves or others.

White Noise - This is the hissing sound that can be heard between radio stations and is sometimes highly magnified through computer programs. Some researchers claim that when examined and listened to closely that discarnate entities, spirit messages and extra-terrestrial correspondence might be audible and recordable. The film of the same name very much brought this term to popular attention.

Whymant, Dr Neville - Endorsed the work of the medium Valiantine and the claim that the ancient Chinese One of Wisdom, Confucius, spoke to this world through Valiantine as an instrument for his words and philosophy.

Wicca - A term for witchcraft, generally practised by white witches, healers and those following the Wiccan way of life.

Willpower - Self control is the exertion of an individual's will on their own personal self, involving control of their actions, thought processes and ultimate behaviour. Usually relevant to the boundaries of acceptability that are appropriate to an individual's place and background. Willpower is the ability of a person to exert authority over personal wants, requirements and needs.

Wilson, Colin - One of the truly brilliant contemporary paranormal writers. Many of Colin Wilson's books deal with mysticism, the paranormal and the afterlife and the way they relate to each other. As he suggests any system of values must ultimately be mystical. One book that may be of particular interest to Spiritualists is called Afterlife, and is a challenging and intriguing overview and insight into aspects of life after death. He also writes with authority in his book The Occult, which is claimed by many experts in the field as a modern-day classic.

Witch - A female who practises witchcraft and the Wiccan way. In history many innocent women who were probably natural mediums were hung for being wise women or witches. It may be of interest to the reader that few were actually burned although some were drowned whilst being 'tested' - this involved plunging them under water for several minutes. If they were still alive when they came up, they were indeed witches, and if they were dead they were considered innocent! (see Warlock).

Witch Doctor - Sometimes called a medicine man. Most of the Native American tribes of America had people who were responsible for upholding the laws and rituals of the tribes, organising ceremonies such as marriage and perhaps most of all communicating with the spirit world for the benefit of all the tribe. Many were also wonderful healers who choose to come back and inspire some healers as their guides today.

Witchcraft - Witchcraft is one of the world's oldest religions and ways of living a life close to nature. Its followers claim it precedes Christianity by many years. Members usually form what is known as a coven led by a high priest or priestess. Most followers of the craft of witchcraft are interested in healing and practising rituals associated to their religion. They are a much misunderstood people in history. Before Spiritualism some mediums would have been attracted to this way of life and in the distant history suffered by being hung based on unfounded claims of evilness.

Wraith - An apparition which is usually the double of someone still living.

Wollaston, Stephen - Also known as Santoshan. Has written many spiritual books and extensively in holistic knowledge of the East and West. One of the co-founders with Glynn Edwards of the Gordon Higginson Fellowship for Integral Spirituality.

Worship - To adore or praise some particular deity.

Wyrd - An ancient Germanic term for your destiny or fate. Beyond your control, dependent on higher spirit intervention.

Xavier, Francisco (1910-2002) - A Spiritist medium from Brazil where he was very famous. In Brazil Spiritualism may be said to have its roots in the works of Allan Kardec, the French Spiritist. Xavier was better known as Chico Xavier. His first experience was to see the spirit of his own mother. He later learned to hear the words of other spirits and used his gift to help many thousands of people to come to the understanding that they had not truly lost loved ones, that they were merely on 'the other side'.

Xenoglossy - A technical term to describe speaking in tongues. Many of the world's religions have individuals within their membership who do speak in languages and dialects that cannot be understood by others and are often not known to themselves when in a conscious state. Some mediums also have this ability though it has not been so popular in more modern times. Dr Ian Stevenson wrote extensively on the subject.

X-ray Vision - Some healers and sensitives suggest they have an ability to see the inner organs and parts of the human body which may be out of balance or need healing.

Yama - The first level of training in yoga which requires you to learn truthfulness, forgiveness and compassion among other areas such as understanding the self and altruism for others.

Yesod - Part of the Kabbala which describes the astral or spirit realms.

Yhva - This mean Jehovah, the god and carer of the ancient Jewish nation.

Yin and Yang - The Chinese ideas of opposites said to be part of all human experiences. Everything has its two sides - good/bad, etc., or its Yin and Yang.

Yoga - Originally a practice of self-discipline and self-awareness, probably part of very old Hindu traditions. Yoga is now popular in many peoples' pathways and in the West has become a popular way to relax and progress as an individual in their life progression.

Yogin - In simple terms describes someone who practises yoga.

Yolande - The guide and control of Madame D'Esperance.

Z

Zammit, Victor J. - A retired lawyer of the Supreme Court of New South Wales and the High Court of Australia. A man who has dedicated much of his life to investigating all areas of the paranormal, particularly Spiritualism, and is highly respected for his work. Worked closely at one time with some important members of various religions but considers himself part of all religions past, present and future, and that nothing is alien to him. Originally suspicious of the New Age movement, a number of psychic and spiritual experiences subsequently led to him researching and reading and passing on his wisdom to others. Today, Victor Zammit is a full-time research source and writer on all areas of empirical evidence for the afterlife and has received great acclaim for one particular book, A Lawyer Presents the Case for the Afterlife. Many have come to rely on his written reports, website comments and other sources of information to keep up to speed with the emerging evidence and suggested links to others actively promoting serious investigation of the truth of the afterlife.

Zen - Part of the life pathway of Buddhism that came to Japan probably from ancient China. It is a form of meditation based on Koans, which lays strong emphasis on learning. With the popularity of martial arts today many practitioners of Judo, and its fighting equivalent Jiu-Jitsu, study Zen and its emphasis on counter-reaction (perhaps similar to the way a boxer counter-punches an opponent to protect himself).

Zener Cards - Used to test individuals' telepathy abilities and other psychic skills. A pack of 25 cards, including five sets of diagrams (circles, signs, rectangles, stars and wavy lines). Greatly used by Professor J. B. Rhine and others in extra-sensory perception tests where an individual must guess the correct cards to allow a measure to be taken of the percentage of psychic ability that may be present in the person being tested.

Zodiac - A term used to describe aspects of the horoscopes within the art of astrology. Also a very important spirit guide especially to Christian Spiritualists (see Christian Spiritualists).

Zohar - Means 'splendour' in ancient Hebrew. Is considered the most important work of the Kabbala (Jewish mysticism) and is a mystical commentary about the Torah - The Five Books of Moses. Within the books is a commentary and discussion of the nature of God, the structure and origin of the world of the universe and the nature of souls, redemption, sin, evil and good, and many other related subject areas.

Zombie - A term that describes the living dead. In some parts of Africa and the Caribbean there is a belief that corpses can be made to walk the Earth plane under the control of a living person or persons, although they have no spirit essence at all.

Zohoastrian - A person who believes there is a struggle between the spirits of darkness and the spirits of goodness. Probably originated from Persian religious texts based on the teachings of Zoroaster.

Useful Addresses

Below is a list of many Spiritualist churches/organisations in the UK and overseas which may be of use to the dictionary reader/researcher.

Many of the churches listed will offer private psychic readings by request with a clairvoyant psychic medium.

Central London
The Greater World Christian Spiritualist Association, 3-5 Conway Street, London, W1P 5HA. Telephone: 0207 436 7555

North London
14 Linnell Road, Edmonton, London, N18 2QW. Tel: 020 8803 8420.
425 Hornsey Road, Islington, London, N19 4DX.
Rochester Square, off Camden Road, London, NW1 9RY. Tel: 020 7435 7446.
95 Green Lanes, Palmers Green, London, N13 4TD. Tel: 01707 876389.
Watling Community Centre, 143 Orange Hill Road, Burnt Oak, Edgware, Middlesex. Tel: 020 8951 1761.
1 Vaughan Road, Harrow, Middlesex, HA1 4DP. Tel: 01923 242156.
656 London Road, Hounslow, Middlesex, TW3 1PG. Tel: 020 8992 5225.
Hounslow Spiritualist Centre, 14-15 Hanworth Terrace, Hounslow, Middlesex, TW3 3TS. Tel: 020 8898 8249.
Civic Centre, High Street, Uxbridge, Middlesex, UB8 1UW. Tel: 01409 221194.

South London
Bennerley Hall, 46 Bennerley Road, Northcote Road, Battersea, London, SW11 6DS. Tel: 020 8265 3383
Hamilton Hall, 211 Balham High Road, Balham, London, SW17 7BQ.
11a North Street, Old Town, Clapham, London, SW4 0HN. Tel: 020 788 5113.
64a Well Hall Road, Eltham, London, SE9 6SH.
The Spiritualist Association of Great Britain, 22 Belgrave Square, London, SW1X

8QB.
St. Michaels Road, Stockwell, London, SW9. Tel: 020 7733 7761.
Two Worlds, 7 The Leather Market, Weston Street, London, SE1 3ER.
95 Wickham Lane, Plumstead, London, SE2 0XW.
Ullswater Road, West Norwood, London, SE27 0AL. Tel: 020 8670 5745.
Kelvedon Road, Fulham, London, SW6 5BP. Tel: 020 7736 7248.

East London and Essex

161 Cumberland Road, Plaistow, London E13.
West Park Crescent, Billericay, CM12 9AS. Tel: 01277 623382.
Primrose Hill, Brentwood, CM14 4LT. Tel: 01638 717379.
The Institute of Spiritualist Mediums, Central Office, 3 Roding Leigh, South Woodham Ferrers, Chelmsford, Essex, CM3 5JZ.
Foresters Hall, Turners Hill, Cheshunt, EN8 9DD. Tel: 01992 621743.
Fennings Chase, off Priory Street, Colchester, CO1 2QG. Tel: 01206 842124.
370-372 High Road, Ilford, Essex, IG1 4AA.
331 Carterhatch Lane, Forty Hill, Enfield, EN1 4AW. Tel: 020 8366 7530.
Third Avenue, Manor Park, Little Ilford, London, E12 6DS.
Shrewsbury Road, Forest Gate, Manor Park, London, E7. Tel: 020 8530 6803.
Psychic News, Clock Cottage, Stansted Hall, Stansted, Essex, CM24 8UD.
The Arthur Findlay College, Stansted Hall, Stansted, Essex, CM24 8UD.
The International Spiritualist Federation, c/o The SNU, General Secretary, Redwoods, Stansted Hall, Stansted, Essex, CM24 8UD.
The Spiritualists' National Union, (incorporating The British Spiritualists' Lyceum Union), Redwoods, Stansted Hall, Stansted, Essex, CM24 8UD.
24 Idmiston Road, Stratford, London E15 1RG.
Vestry Road, Walthamstow, London, E17 9RN. Tel: 020 8520 8610.
Walthamstow Lyceum, 39 Coleridge Road, Walthamstow, London E17 6QX.
Westborough Road, Hildaville Drive, Westcliff-on-Sea, Essex, SS0 9PZ. Tel: 01702 510338.
9 Grove Crescent, South Woodford, London, E18 2JR.. Tel: 020 8989 6149.

West London

The Cottage, Woodhurst Road, Acton, London, W3 6SL. Tel: 020 8896 0184.
66-68 Uxbridge Road, Ealing, London, W13 8RA. Tel: 020 8567 0403.
The White Eagle Lodge (London), 9 St Mary Abbots Place, Kensington, London, W8 6LS.

The Midlands

55 Baden Powell Road, Chesterfield, Derbyshire, S40 2SL. Tel: 01246 452295.
Bridge Road, Coalville, Leicester. Tel: 01530 230140.
18 Charnwood Street, Derby. Tel: 01332 386204.
Rear of 2a Forester Street, Derby, DE1 1PP. Tel: 01332 523587.
Edward Road, Hill Top, Eastwood, Nottinghamshire. Tel: 01773 763671.
Low Moor Road, Kirkby in Ashfield, Nottinghamshire NG17 7BH. Tel: 01623 721905.
Leicester Progressive, 4 St. James Street, Lee Circle, Leicester, LE1 3SU. Tel: 0116 253 6098.

The Lynwood Fellowship, Royes Ridge, 1 Plough Hill, Calstor, Lincoln, LN7 6UR.
The Lynwood Fellowship, 36 Lady Frances Drive, Market Rasen, Lincoln, LN8 3PH,
Broad Street, Long Eaton, Nottinghamshire, NG10 1JH. Tel: 0115 849 2682.
Steeple Row, Loughborough, Leicestershire, LE11 1UX. Tel: 01509 237589.
Dallas Street, Mansfield, Nottinghamshire. Tel: 01623 471228.
1a Beaconsfield Street, Hyson Green, Nottingham, NG7 6FD. Tel: 0115 840 9057.
Cambridge Avenue, Millfield, Peterborough, Cambridgeshire, PE1 2JF. Tel: 01733
243766.
Argyll Road, Ripley, Derbyshire. Tel: 01773 743054.
West Bridgford Spiritual Church, Bridgford Road, West Bridgford, Nottingham. Tel:
0117 945 5927.
37 George Street, Worksop, Nottinghamshire, S80 1QJ. Tel: 0114 248 6987.
5 Springfield Road, Kings Heath, Birmingham, B14 7DT. Tel: 0121 444 5195.
The Quinborne Community Centre, Ridgeacre Road, Quinton, Birmingham,
B32 2TW. Tel: 01384 232267.
Revival Street, Bloxwich, Walsall, West Midlands. Tel: 01922 422084.
Church Road, Catshill, Bromsgrove, Worcestershire, B61 0JY. Tel: 01527 872317.
High Street, Brownhills, Walsall, West Midlands, WS8 6HE. Tel: 01902 397311.
Rear of 23 Market Street, Hednesford, Cannock, Staffordshire. Tel: 01543 422974.
73-83 Eagle Street, Foleshill, Coventry, CV1 4GP. Tel: 024 7646 2412.
Parkside, Coventry, CV6 2NE. Tel: 024 7465 9286.
Pinfold Street Extension, Darlaston, West Midlands, WS10 8PU. Tel: 0121 520 3376.
Oat Street Chapel, Evesham, Worcestershire. Tel: 01386 833208.
60-62 King Street, Fenton, Stoke on Trent, ST4 3ET. Tel: 01782 846692.
The Phoenix Centre, Stoke on Trent, Avenue Road, Shelton, Stoke on Trent. Tel:
01782 833352.
1-2 Holly Street, Leamington Spa, Warwickshire, CV32 4TN. Tel: 01789 470058.
Normacot Road, Longton, Stoke on Trent, ST3 1PL. Tel: 01782 595481.
Norman Avenue, Nuneaton, Warwickshire, CV11 5NZ. Tel: 024 7634 1097.
139 Easemore Road, Redditch B98 8HU. Tel: 01527 870040 or 01905 796175.
Shirley Institute, Church Road, Shirley, Solihull, West Midlands. Tel: 0121 733 2385.
David Jones Centre, 96a Stone Road, Stafford, ST16 2RZ. Tel: 01889 808460.
Union Street, Stourbridge, DY8 1PJ. Tel: 01384 396955.
Sutton Coldfield Spiritualist Church, Kenelm Road, Sutton Coldfield, B73 6HD.
Telephone: 0121 354 3266
Marmion Street, Tamworth, Staffordshire, B79 7JG. Tel: 01827 68782.
St James Hall, Farm Lane. Stirchley Village, Telford, Shropshire, TF3 1DY. Tel: 01952
591187.
Caldmore Road, Walsall, West Midlands, WS1 3NQ. Tel: 01922 629025.
Regent Street, Wellington, Telford, Shropshire. Tel: 01952 243362.
Waterloo Road, Wolverhampton, WV7 4QU. Tel: 01902 313694.

North of England

Clarendon Avenue, Stockport Road, Altrincham, Cheshire, WA15 8HD. Tel: 0161
945 1870.
Burlington Street, Ashton under Lyne, Tameside. Tel: 0161 231 2996.
21 Bradford Street, Bolton, Lancashire, BL2 1HT. Tel: 01204 430053.
Russell Street, Bury, Lancashire, BL9 5AT. Tel: 0161 654 9282.
15 Park Road, Congleton, Cheshire, CW12 1DS. Tel: 01782 518235.

4-6 Adelaide Street, Crewe, Cheshire. Tel: 01270 662944.

14-16 New Road, Dearnley, Littleborough, Lancashire, OL15 8LX. Tel: 01706 377122.

Annan Street, Denton, Manchester, M34 3FX. Tel: 0161 336 1468.

7 Jones Street, Hadfield, Hyde, Cheshire, SK14 7BZ. Tel: 01457 865628.

Chorley New Road, Horwich, Bolton, Lancashire. Tel: 01204 695984.

Great Norbury Street, Hyde, SK14 1HX. Tel: 0161 320 7658.

Cumberland Street, Macclesfield, Cheshire, SK10 1DD. Tel: 01625 617724.

2 Alexandra Road South, Whalley Range, Manchester, M16 8ER. Tel: 0161 227 9702.

Hadfield Street, Northwich, Cheshire, CW9 5LU. Tel: 01606 48586.

157-159 Ashton Road, Oldham, Lancashire. Tel: 0161 630 6043.

Cross Lane, Liverpool Street, Salford, Lancashire, M5 4HH. Tel: 01253 352414.

Duke Street, off Beal Lane, Shaw, Oldham, Lancashire, OL2 8PA. Tel: 0161 6781 989.

1 Mount Grove, Oxton, Birkenhead, Wirral, Merseyside, CH42 2UJ. Tel: 0151 512 3609.

14 Daulby Street, Liverpool, L3 5NX. Tel: 0151 524 0284.

61 Ashridge Street, Runcorn, Cheshire, WA7 1HU. Tel: 01928 563462.

20-22 Charles Street, St Helens, Merseyside, WA10 1LH. Tel: 01744 451924.

61 Withens Lane, Wallasey, Merseyside, CH45 7NE. Tel: 0151 677 8786.

66 Academy Street, Warrington, WA1 2BQ. Tel: 01925 658313.

28 South Road, Waterloo, Liverpool, Merseyside, L22 5PQ. Tel: 0151 931 3777.

Lacey Street, Widnes, Cheshire. Tel: 07901 718722.

Brompton Street, Wigan, Lancashire. Tel: 01942 864550.

St. Peter Street, Blackburn, BB2 2HL. Tel: 01254 691078.

71 Albert Road, Blackpool, Lancashire, FY1 4PW.

Stanley Street, Burnley, BB1 2HH. Tel: 01282 773868.

93 Beach Road, Cleveleys, Lancashire. Tel: 01253 777538.

Greenacre Street, Clitheroe, Lancashire, BB7 1ED. Tel: 01200 424345.

59 Spring Lane, Colne, Lancashire, BB8 9BD. Tel: 01282 614970.

Britten Hall, Bulk Road, Lancaster. Tel: 01524 844971.

West End Road, Morecambe, Lancashire. Tel: 01524 425529.

Moor Lane, Preston, Lancashire. Tel: 01257 232848.

68/70 Newchurch Road, Rawtenstall, Rossendale, Lancashire. Tel: 01706 220010.

Pensioners Hall, St. Albans Road, St. Annes on Sea, Lancashire, FY8 1XD. Tel: 01772 466604.

Martin Street, Brighouse, West Yorkshire, HD6 1DA. Tel: 01274 883687.

Lower Oxford Street, Castleford, West Yorkshire, WF10 4AQ. Tel: 01977 683456.

35-39 Duncombe Street, Grimsby, North East Lincolnshire, DN32 7SG. Tel: 01472 354068.

Old Leeds Road, Huddersfield, West Yorkshire, HD1 1SG. Tel: 01484 311785.

83 Folkestone Street, Hull, East Yorkshire, HU5 2TD. Tel: 07949 513451.

Knaresborough House, High Street, Knaresborough, North Yorkshire, HG5 0MW. Tel: 01423 866688.

Zoar Street, Morley, Leeds, West Yorkshire, LS27 8JB. Tel: 0113 2380 376.

172/174 Castleford Road, Normanton, West Yorkshire. Tel: 01924 250567.

Broadheads Yard, Ventnor Way, Ossett, WF5 8PA. Tel: 01924 263200.

Harp Road, Longwood, Huddersfield, West Yorkshire. Tel: 01484 543373.

7 Moorhead Lane, Saltaire, Shipley, West Yorkshire, BD18 4JH. Tel: 01274 878418.

5 Queen Street, Scarborough, YO11 1HA. Tel: 01723 369475.

2 Romille Street, off Sackville Street, Skipton, North Yorkshire. Tel: 01576 795454.

7-9 Wilton Rise, Holgate, York, YO2 4BT. Tel: 01904 642390.

Pitt Street West, Barnsley, South Yorkshire, S70 1BB.

Church Street, Brierley, Barnsley, South Yorkshire. Tel: 01226 712636.

Catherine Street, Doncaster, South Yorkshire, DN1 3PS. Tel: 01302 367117.

Bank Street, Mexborough, South Yorkshire, S64 9LL. Tel: 01709 740110.

Newholme Drive, Moorends, Doncaster, DN8 4TB. Tel: 01405 817187.

109 Whitham Road, Broomhill, Sheffield, South Yorkshire, S10 2SL. Tel: 0114 266 4025.

Bold Street, Sheffield, South Yorkshire, S9 2LR. Tel: 0114 265 7185.

1 Clarkson Street, Sheffield, South Yorkshire, S10 1TQ. Tel: 0114 255 1543 & 01709 372215.

315 Shirland Lane, Darnall, Sheffield, South Yorkshire, S9 3FN. Tel: 0114 261 8727.

Station Road, Stainforth, Doncaster, South Yorkshire. Tel: 01302 888363.

Edlington Lane, Warmsworth, Doncaster, South Yorkshire. Tel: 01302 866435.

6 Barnsley Road, Wath on Dearne, Rotherham, South Yorkshire, S63 7PY. Tel: 01709 889043.

Hawthorn Road, Ashington, Northumberland. Tel: 01670 852695.

Back Ravensworth Street, Bedlington Street, Bedlington, Northumberland. Tel: 01670 361030.

Chapel Road, Billingham, Cleveland, TS23 1DX. Tel: 01642 881211.

1a Mitchell Street, Birtley, Co Durham, DH3 1EP. Tel: 0191 410 6703.

Front Street, Craghead, Stanley, Durham, DH9 6DS. Tel: 01207 233782.

The Old Chapel, Denmark Street, Darlington, Co Durham. Tel: 01748 834719.

2 John Street, Durham City, Co Durham, DH1 4DE.

Rectory Hall, St. Cuthberts Place, Gateshead, NE8 1TB. Tel: 0191 477 8588.

Yoden Way, Horden, Peterlee, Co Durham. Tel: 0191 5865 952.

Monkton Road, Jarrow, Tyne and Wear, NE32 3LS. Tel: 0191 421 4920.

115 Borough Road, Middlesbrough, Cleveland, TS1 3AN.

Newcastle Road, Sunderland, SR5 1NA. Tel: 0191 516 0722.

16-18 Tosson Terrace, Heaton, Newcastle upon Tyne, NE6 5LX. Tel: 0191 267 6527.

Rippon Hall, 42 Stanley Street West, North Shields, Tyne and Wear. Tel: 0191 259 6844.

Chapel Row, Philadelphia, Houghton le Spring, Tyne and Wear, DH4 4JB. Tel: 0191 416 5513.

Community Centre, Windsor Road, Saltburn, Cleveland. Tel: 01287 207274.

Middleton Road, Shildon, Co Durham, DL14 1NN. Tel: 01388 774330.

33 Beach Road, South Shields, Tyne and Wear. Tel/Fax: 0191 456 4166.

St Andrews Lane, Spennymoor, Co Durham, DL16 6NG. Tel: 01388 818748.

1 Grange Terrace, Stockton Road, Sunderland, SR2 7DF.

10 South Parade, Whitley Bay, Tyne and Wear, NE26 2RG. Tel: 0191 252 8395.

South of England

177 Canterbury Street, Gillingham, Kent, ME7 5TU. Tel: 01634 576186.

19 Clarence Place, Gravesend, Kent DA12 1LD.

St. Michael's Community Centre, Wrotham Road, Welling, Kent. Tel: 020 8303 6832.

Surrey Road, off High Street, West Wickham, Kent, BR4 0JU. Tel: 020 8777 9375.

8-9 Portland Place, Hastings, East Sussex, TN38 1QN. Tel: 01424 218594.

Brighton Brotherhood Gate, 21c St James's Street, Brighton, East Sussex, BN2 1RF.

Tel: 01273 683589

Edward Street, Brighton, East Sussex, BN2 2JR. Tel: 01273 571168 or 01273 683088.

Amersham Common Village Hall, White Lion Road, Amersham, Buckinghamshire. Tel: 01753 886553.

Mount Street, Aylesbury, Buckinghamshire. Tel: 01869 243896.

Angel Close, Windmill Road, Hampton Hill, TW12 1RH. Tel: 020 8979 2078.

7 Sudley Road, Bognor Regis, West Sussex, PO21 1EJ. Tel: 01243 849164.

Three Bridges Spiritualist Church, 10 New Street, Three Bridges, Crawley, West Sussex. Tel: 01293 822586.

Littlehampton & Rustington, Scout Hall, Church Road, Rustington, West Sussex, BN16 3NN. Tel: 01903 721118.

Capel Lane, Gossops Green, Crawley, West Sussex, RH11 8HL. Tel: 01293 538599 or 0144 424 3528.

214 Morden Road, Morden, Surrey, SW19 3BY. Tel: 020 8764 2341.

The Halfway, Hersham Road, Walton on Thames, Surrey, KT12 1RW. Tel: 01932 562891 or 01932 567221.

St. Barnabas Road, Sutton, Surrey, SM1 4NP. Tel: 01372 379489.

112 Gordon Road, Camberley, Surrey, GU15 2JQ. Tel: 01344 641318.

Villiers Road, Kingston on Thames, Surrey. Tel: 020 8404 7745.

York Lodge, 81 Baker Street, Reading, RG1 7XY. Tel: 0118 950 7281.

Adelaide Square, off Kings Road, Windsor, Berkshire, SL4 2AQ. Tel: 01753 851227.

Friends Hall, 55 Lord Street, Hoddesdon, Hertfordshire. Tel: 01992 462006.

Vasanta Hall, 6 Gernon Walk, Letchworth, Hertfordshire, SG6 3HW.

40 Granville Road, St Albans, Hertfordshire. Tel: 01727 840170.

Marsden Green, off Marsden Road, Welwyn Garden City, Hertfordshire. Tel: 01707 690649.

Friends Meeting House, St. Johns Street, Bury St. Edmunds, Suffolk. Tel: 01284 750811.

Myers Memorial Hall, 5 Thompsons Lane, Cambridge, CB5 8AQ.

28 Victoria Street, Basingstoke, RG21 3BT. Tel: 01256 427819.

16 Bath Road, Bournemouth, Dorset, BH1 2PE. Tel: 01202 551751 or 01202 434446.

Chichester, Venue under review. Tel: 01243 771864 for details.

196b Barrack Road, Christchurch, BH23 2BQ. Tel: 01202 429625 or 01202 463985.

Newport Road, Cowes, Isle of Wight. Tel: 01983 529653.

183 Forton Road, Gosport, PO12 3HB. Tel: 023 9236 7263.

Brockhampton Lane, Havant, PO9 1JB. Tel: 02392 358367.

Hythe and Dibden Parish Hall, West Street, Hythe, Southampton, Hampshire. Tel: 023 8089 2262.

17 Victoria Road, Parkstone, Poole, BH12 3BA. Tel: 01202 566332.

73a Victoria Road South, Southsea, PO5 2BU. Tel: 02392 663993.

106 Wilton Road, Salisbury SP2 7JJ. Tel: 01722 336784.

Bitterne Road, Bitterne, Southampton, SO18 1DR. Tel: 023 8044 2672.

10 Grove Road, Shirley, Southampton, SO1 3GG. Tel: 023 8084 6954 or 023 8073 3748.

641 Portswood Road, Swaythling, Southampton, SO17 3SN. Tel: 023 804 8959.

Scout Hall, Porchester Road, Woolston, Southampton, Hampshire. Tel: 023 8049 0223.

8a Rumbridge Street, Totton, Southampton, SO40 6DP. Tel: 023 8066 8145.

193 Aldershot Road, Crookham Crossroads, Church Crookham, Fleet, Hampshire, GU13 0JS. Tel: 01420 538069.

Priory Hall, Love Lane, Andover, Hampshire. Tel: 01264 392138.

16 Old Orchard Street, Manvers Place, Bath, Avon, BA1 1JU. Tel: 01225 463579.

18 Hart Street, Bideford, Devon, EX39 2LB. Tel: 01769 550984.

74 Chessel Street, Bedminster, Bristol, BS3 3DN. Tel: 0117 964 6870.

31 Belmont Road, St. Andrews, Bristol, BS6 5AW. Tel: 0117 909 2593.

St John Hall, Wick Road, Brislington, Bristol, Avon. Tel: 0117 985 0880.

St Johns Ambulance Hall, Tilling Road, Horfield, Bristol, Avon. Tel: 0117 949 6964.

Surrey House, 10 Surrey Street, off Broadmead, Bristol. Tel: 07741 000692.

Cairns Road, Westbury Park, Bristol, BS6 7TH. Tel: 0117 977 1629.

Bennington Street, Cheltenham, GL50 4ED. Tel: 01386 831960.

Kingsley Hall, Old Street, Clevedon, Somerset. Tel: 01275 874830.

2a Brunswick Square, Gloucester, GL1 1UG. Tel: 01452 305861.

The Friends Meeting House, King Street, Melksham, SN12 6HT. Tel: 01373 722400.

East Street, Newton Abbot, Devon, TQ12 1AQ. Tel: 07788 826510.

Manor Corner, Preston, Paignton, Devon, TQ3 2JB. Tel: 01803 525933.

Keppel Place, Stoke, Plymouth, PL2 1AX. Tel: 01752 290406.

Pearson Road, Mutley, Plymouth, Devon, PL4 7DH. Tel: 01752 783064.

31 Devizes Road, Swindon, Wiltshire, SN1 4BG. Tel: 01793 530334.

The Noah's Ark Society, 7 Sheen Close, Grange Park, Swindon, SN5 6JF.

Staplegrove Village Hall, Staplegrove Road, Taunton, Somerset.

Town Hall, The Platt, Wadebridge, Cornwall, PL27 7AB. Tel: 01208 75558 or 01208 841732.

Weston Super Mare Spiritualist National Church, 2a Stafford Road, Weston Super Mare, BS23 3BW. Tel: 01934 510710.

21 Ashburnham Road, Bedford, MK40 1DX. Tel: 01234 210381.

Whinbush Road, Hitchin, SG5 1PZ. Tel: 01462 451334 or 01234 262414.

Castle Moat Road, Huntingdon, Cambridgeshire, PE18 6PG. Tel: 01385 772217.

St. Peters Avenue, Kettering, NN16 9RD. Tel: 01604 402943.

East of England

Littleport Village Hall, Victoria Street, Littleport, Ely. Tel: 01353 860696.

13 Gordon Road, Lowestoft, Suffolk. Tel: 01502 568243.

Village Hall, Station Road, Hopton, Great Yarmouth, NR31 9BE. Tel: 01502 731642.

Chapelfield North, Norwich, Norfolk NR2 1NY.

Wales

Hafan-y-Coed Spiritual Development Centre, Heol Tawe, Abercrave, Swansea, SA9 1TJ. Tel: 01639 730985.

Ambulance Hall, Depot Road, Aberdare, Mid Glamorgan. Tel: 01645 882331.

Pandy Park, Aberkenfig, Bridgend, Mid Glamorgan. Tel: 01639 778057.

Buttrills Road, Barry, Vale of Glamorgan, CF6 2SS. Tel: 029 2053 0294.

204 High Street, Blackwood, Gwent. Tel: 01443 833577.

The Rhiw, Bridgend, Mid Glamorgan, CF31 3BL. Tel: 01446 790294.

20 Park Grove, Cardiff, South Glamorgan, CF1 3BN.

17 Woodland Road, Colwyn Bay, Clwyd, LL29 7DH. Tel: 01492 540958.

1 Fountain Street, Ferndale, Rhondda, Mid Glamorgan. Tel: 01443 755234.

St. Margarets, Lower Thomas Street, Merthyr Tydfil, Twynyrodyn, Mid Glamorgan. Tel: 01685 375362.

Tramroadside North, Merthyr Tydfil, Mid Glamorgan. Tel: 01443 690990.

29 Charles Street, Newport, NP9 1JT.

43 Queen Street, Pembroke Dock, Dyfed. Tel: 01348 874452.

1 Tydraw Place, Port Talbot, West Glamorgan, SA13 1JZ. Tel: 01639 793720 or 01639 793027.

Gwynfa Villa, off Thorpe Street, Rhyl, LL18 3LR.

Cwrch-y-Gwas Road, Treforest, Pontypridd, Mid Glamorgan. Tel: 01443 491071.

Wyndham Street, Troedyrhiw, Merthyr Tydfil, Mid Glamorgan. Tel: 01443 693769.

St. Davids Road, Ystalyfera, Swansea, West Glamorgan. Tel: 01639 844187.

Scotland

Stephen House, 71 Dee Street, Aberdeen, AB1 2EE. Tel: 01224 574916.

37 Fraser Place, Aberdeen, AB25 3TY. Tel: 01224 622417.

20-22 Commerce Street, Arbroath, DD11 1NB. Tel: 01241 875979.

10 Alloway Place, Ayr, KA7 2AA. Tel: 01292 266805.

Dundee Church of the Spirit, 142 Nethergate, Dundee, Tayside, DD1 4EA. Tel: 01382 226149.

St Davids Rooms, Nethergate, Dundee, Tayside. Tel: 01382 226975.

3 Lady Campbells Walk, Dunfermline, Fife, KY12 0TL. Tel: 01383 417798.

34 Albany Street, Edinburgh, EH1 3QH. Tel: 0131 556 1749.

Edinburgh Association of Spiritualists, 246 Morrison Street, Edinburgh, EH5 8DT. Tel: 01383 626175.

8 Burnhead Lane, Falkirk, FY1 1UG. Tel: 01324 715111.

64 Berkeley Street, Glasgow, G3 7DS. Tel: 0141 221 6201.

19 Park Road, Hamilton, Lanarkshire, ML3 6PD. Tel: 01698 284859.

Smithton Hall, Sinclair Terrace, Smithton, Inverness, IV2 7DY. Tel: 01463 790390.

30 Old Mill Road, Kilmarnock, Ayrshire. Tel: 01292 314559.

Feuars Hall, 145 Commercial Street, Kirkcaldy, KY1 2NS. Tel: 01592 262955.

Victoria House, 13 Kirk Wynd, Kirkcaldy, Fife. Tel: 01592 643645.

Glenburn Community Centre, Paisley. Tel: 0141 884 3232.

40 Methven Buildings, Newrow, Perth, PH1 5OA. Tel: 01738 636416.

Freefield Centre, North Road, Lerwick, Shetland.

27 King Street, Stirling, FK8 1DN. Tel: 01786 474043.

Ireland

Belfast Spiritualist Church SNU Affiliated, 134 Malone Avenue, Lisburn Road, Belfast, Antrim. Tel: 028 9081 8078.

Belfast Spiritualist Fellowship Group, 44 Bainsmore Drive, Belfast, Northern Ireland, BT13 3FF.

KB Spiritualist Society of Ireland, 14 Pine Tree Crescent, Garrynisk, Tallacht, Dublin 24.

Isle of Wight

Belvedere Street, Ryde, Isle of Wight PO33 2JW. Tel: 01983 612189

8 Victoria Street, Ventnor, Isle of Wight PO38 1ET.

Tel: 01983 731 748

Australia
Canberra
Canberra Spiritualist Assoc Inc, The Griffin Centre, ACT. Tel: (02) 6231 3300.
Diaura Centre, P.O. Box 978, Woden, ACT, 26. Tel: 02 6296 2489.
Melba Community Hall, The Melba Shopping Centre, Chinner Crescent, Melba. Tel: (02) 6242 6347 or (02) 6295 1086.
South Canberra Spiritualist Church, Hughes Community Centre, Hughes. Tel: (02) 6287 4000.

New South Wales
Berkshire Park Spiritualist Church, 34 First Street, Bershire Park, NSW. Tel: (02) 9589 1082.
Bexley North Spiritualist Church, 38/165 Belmore Road, Riverwood, Bexley North, NSW, 2210. Tel: (02) 534-4637.
Blacktown Spiritual Centre, Blacktown North Public School, Bessemer Street, Blacktown, NSW, 2148. Tel: (02) 9671 1861 or 0422 713 140.
Bowral Spiritual Church, 73 Mooreland Road, Tahmoor, NSW, 2573. Tel: (02) 589 1082.
Chatswood Spiritual Church, Girl Guides Hall, Thompson Avenue, Artarmon, NSW, 2064. Tel: (02) 9971 5584.
Church of United Spiritualism of Australia, 25 Denison Street Newcastle West. Tel: (04) 9422 951.
Cronulla Spiritualist Church, Senior Citizens' Hall, Port Hacking Road, Caringbah, 22. Tel: (02) 9545 0832.
Drummoyne Gladesville Spiritualist Centre, 10 Cometrowe Street, Drummoyne Community, Sydney. Tel: (02) 9774 4862.
Enmore Spiritualist Church, 2 London Street, Enmore, NSW, 2042. Tel: (02) 9519 6436.
Everyone's Spiritual Centre, 172 Lawson St, Hamilton. Tel: (04) 926 2104.
Everyone's Spiritual Church Association, Corner Moorhead and De Vitre Streets, Lambton, Newcastle. Tel: (02) 4968 3409.
Hobart Community Hall, Creek Road, Lenah Valley, Hobart, Tasmania. Tel: (03) 6272 8503.
Lighthouse Spiritual Centre, 494 Windsor Road, Baulkham Hills, Sydney, NSW, 2153. Tel: (02) 968 62230.
Newcastle Spiritualist Church Inc, 3 Swan Street, Newcastle, NSW, 2300. Tel: (02) 4926 3402.
Nowra Christian Spiritualist Church, Berry Street, Nowra, NSW 2540.
Our Community Spiritual Church, 57 Peppertree Drive, Erskine Park, NSW, 2759. Tel: (02) 9835 1390. Mobile: 0425 209872.
Sutherland Spiritual Church, Multi Purpose Centre, Flora Street, Sutherland. Tel: (02) 9589 1082.
The Centre of Love, Light and Healing, P.O. Box 351, Riverwood, NSW, 22. Tel: (04) 1841 5807.
The Soul Centre Sydney, Level 1, 38 Norton Street, Leichhardt, NSW, 2040. Tel: 9518 0170. Mobile: 0404 258 949

Werrington Spiritualist Church, Victoria Cottage, Robuck Street, Werrington. Tel: (04) 721 2211.

Northern Territory

Heavenly Signpost Healing Centre, Sho 2, Bonanni Arcade, Gregory Terrace. Tel: (08) 895 24654.

Queensland

Beerwah Spiritual Church (ACSOA), Masonic Lodge, Peachester Road, Beewah. Tel: (07) 5496 3584.

Bribie Island Cultural Spiritual Group, 36 Banya Street, Bongaree, Bribie Island. Tel: (07) 3408 3924 or (07) 5429-5449.

Bridge of Light, Healing & Counselling Centre, Callide Street, Biloela. Tel: (07) 4992 4260.

Brisbane City Spiritual Church, 288 Boundary Road, Springhill. Tel: (07) 3832 6023.

Brisbane Spiritual Church, 228 Boundary Street, Spring Hill, Brisbane, 40. Tel: (07) 3832 6023.

Caboolture Christian Spiritualist Church, 5 Dux Street, Caboolture, 4510. Tel: (07) 5498 9125 or (07) 5497 4629.

Cairns Spiritual Church of Healing & Meditation, Spiritual Centre, Greenslopes Street, Cairns. Tel: (07) 4055 1391.

Cairns Spiritualist Group, Community Hall, Corner Greenslopes & Little Street, Eagle Hill. Tel: (07) 4034 3408.

Centre of Guiding Light, 5 Private Court, Edens Landing. Tel: (07) 3805 3007.

Church of United Spiritualism of Australia, corner Hancock and Lagoon Street, Sandgate. Tel: 3822 1406.

Church of United Spiritualism of Australia, CCSA Hall, Nutley Street, Caloundra. Tel: 5497 0539.

Coomera Christian Spiritual Church (ACSCOA), School of Arts Hall, Reserve Road, Upper Coomera. Tel: 0755-450484.

CWA Hall, Torquay Road, Pialba Qld. Tel: (07) 4125 7456.

Hervey Bay/Maryborough Spiritual Centre, Community Centre-Botanical Gardens, Elizabeth Street, Urangan, Hervey Bay. Tel: (07) 4128 3875.

Hinterland Church for Spiritual Growth Inc. (ACSCOA), Nerang Community Hall, 34 Price Street, Nerang, Gold Coast, 4211. Tel: (07) 5572 1133 or 0418 764 491.

Ipswich Christian Spiritual Church, The Blair State School, corner Crib and Burnett Street, Sadliers Crossing. Tel: (07) 5464 6989 or 0412 134 356.

Maroochydore Spiritual Church, Memorial Avenue, Maroochydore. Tel: (07) 5479 1095.

Noosa and District Spiritualist Church, Tinbeerwah Hall, corner Sunrise Road & Cooroy Noosa Road, Tinbeerwah. P.O. Box 747, Tewantin, QLD, 4565. Tel: (07) 5485 1138.

Redlands Christian Spiritual Centre, 305 Old Cleveland Road East, Capalaba. Tel: (07) 3245 1594.

Salisbury Centre for Personal Growth, 183 Lillian Avenue, Salisbury. Tel: (07) 3274 4975.

South Coast & Hinterland Spiritualist Church, Old Post Office Building, Mudgeeraba. Tel: (07) 5522 9572.

Southside Spiritual Haven, (Australian Affiliated Spiritual Association), Progress

Hall,
corner Railway Parade & Garfield Road, Woodridge, Qld, 4114. Tel: (07) 3299 4326 or (07) 3388 2030.

Sunshine Coast Spiritualist Church, Masonic Lodge, corner Third Avenue & Arthur Street, Caloundra. Tel: (074)4917203.

The Centre of Spiritual Light Inc, Progress Hall, Coral Street, Loganlea. Tel: (04) 0759 8672.

The Christian Spiritual Fellowship, Municipal Hall, corner Bay Terrace & Cedar Street, Wynnum. Tel: (07) 3206.0495.

The Community Centre for Personal Growth, 183 Lillian Ave, P.O. Box 416, Salisbury, Qld, 4107. Tel: (07) 3274 4975.

The Guiding Light Centre, Heritage Hut, Mortimor Road, Acacia Ridge, Brisbane, Queensland, 4110. Tel: (07) 3275 3836 or 0408 072 393.

The Inner Light Centre, 153 lindah Road, Tinana, 46. Tel: (07) 4123 1552.

The Light Within Centre, 11 Basswood Court, Albany Creek. Tel: (07) 3264 5575.

The Ministry Of Angels Christian Spiritualist Church, Masonic Hall, Watson Street, Hervey Bay, Pialbo. Tel: (07) 4124 0360 or (07) 4125 6655.

The Sanctuary of Inner Peace (ACSCOA), Tugun Community Centre, Coolangatta Road, Tugan, Gold Coast. Tel: (07) 5576 4346.

The South Burnett Spiritualist Church, CWA Hall, Fitzroy Street, Nanango. Tel: (07) 4162 2027.

The Spiritual People's Church, Community Centre, Lawson Street, Southport, Gold Coast. Tel: (07) 5522 9572.

Tweed Lighthouse Christian Spiritualist Church, HACC Centre, Heffron Street, South Tweed Heads. Tel: (07) 5533 1015 or 0408 985 993.

United Spiritualism of Australia, The Old Church Willis Road Bli Bli. Tel: (07) 5428 2664.

United Spiritualism of Australia, Buffalo Lodge, 21 Price Street, Nambour. Tel: (07) 5498 8384.

United Spiritualism of Australia, Caboolture. Tel: (07) 5498 3734.

United Spiritualism of Australia, Dandina House Boat Harbour Drive, Torquay, Hervey Bay. Tel: (07) 4125 7456.

Southern Australia

Elizabeth Spiritualist Church, corner Hogarth & Goodman Road, Elizabeth South, 5112. Tel: (08) 8252 2110.

New Age Spiritual Mission Inc, The Rosa Tingey Centre, 38 Palmerston Road, Unley, 5061. Tel: (08) 8172 0515.

Northfield Spiritualist Church, 36 West Avenue, Northfield 5109. Tel: (08) 8261 7250.

Parkholme Spiritualist Centre, 638 Marion Road, Parkholme. Tel: (08) 8295 4706.

Spiritual Mission of Noarlunga, Institute Building, Patapinda Road, Old Noarlunga. Tel: (07) 8186 1729.

St John's Spiritualist Church, 271 Carrington Street, Adelaide SA, 5000. Tel: (08) 8260 1102.

The New Age Spiritualist Mission, 38 Palmerston Road, Unley. Tel: (08) 8261 8806 or (08) 8260 1619.

Victoria

A. B.Victorian Spiritualists' Union Inc, 71-73 A'Beckett Street, Melbourne. Tel: (613) 9663 6121.

Aquarian Spiritualist Church, Rowville. Tel: (03) 9763 2858.

Aquarian Spiritual Learning Centre, 13 Lucy Court, Narre Warren North, 3804. Tel: (03) 9796 7868.

Berwick Spiritualist Church, Berwick Masonic Hall, 106 High Street, Berwick. Tel: (03) 9702 1662.

Boronia Spiritual Centre, Suite 3, 13/15 Chandler Road, Boronia. Tel: (03) 9762 8453.

Brunswick Spiritual Lyceum Church, 259 Victoria St, Brunswick, 3056. Tel: (03) 9387 5515 or (03) 9354 7710.

Church of Peace and Enlightenment, 11 Moyle Street, Ballarat. Tel: (03) 5342 0822.

Church of the Resurrected Life, 523 Centre Road, Bentleigh. Tel: (03) 563 9400.

Church of Spiritual Unity Inc., Fairfield Community Centre, 121 Station Street, Fairfield, Preston. Tel: (03) 9350 6882.

Cosmic Awareness and Healing Centre, 7 Willmette Court, Lilydale. Tel: (03) 9735 4254.

Fawkner Spiritualist Church, Fawkner Community Centre, Jukes Road, Fawkner, 3060. Tel: (03) 9359 1791.

Gippsland Spiritualist Centre Inc, P.O. Box 85, Lang Lang, 3984. Tel: (03) 97 5615.

Golden Dolphin Healing and Spiritualist Centre, Community Centre, Chirnside Park. Tel: (03) 5964 6179.

Golden Light Spiritualist Centre Inc, Manchester Unity Hall, 8 Main Street, Blackburn, 3130. Tel: (03) 9723 7328.

Heavenly Light Spiritualist Church, Derby Street, Pascoe Vale South. Tel: (07) 9350 6882.

Hobart Community Hall, Creek Road, Lenah Valley, Hobart, Tasmania. Tel: (03) 6272 8503.

Inner Light Centre, 11 Kerferd Street, Coburg. Tel: (03) 9350 6240.

Latrobe Valley Spiritualist Church & Yoorami Healing Centre, 2 Avondale Road, Morwell, 3840. Tel: (03) 5134 3253.

Lilydale and District Spiritualist Church, Tapscott Girl Guides Hall, Cambridge Road,
Montrose, 3765. Tel: (03) 9725 3114.

Malvern Healing and Psychic Centre, Manchester Unity Hall, Valetta Street, Malvern, 3144. Tel: (03) 9478 6693.

Monash Spiritualist Centre Inc, Hughesdale Community Centre, corner Poath & Kangaroo Road, Hughesdale, 3166. Tel: (03) 9702 1885.

Pastel Realm, 374 Dorset Road, Boronia, 3155. Tel: (03) 9762 5791.

Pocket Full of Rainbows, Main Road, Upwey. Tel: (03) 9752 6900.

Seaford Spiritual and Healing Centre Inc, Community Hall, Station Street, Seaford, 3198. Tel: (03) 9789 2020 or (03) 5977 7874.

Shangri-La Healing Sanctuary, P.O. Box 29, Seville. Tel: (03) 5964 7224.

Shepparton Spiritual Centre Inc, Baringa Blind Centre, corner Channel Road & Archer Street, Shepparton, 3630. Tel: (03) 5831 4497.

Southern Peninsula Spiritual Church, Community Hall, corner Verdon & Hodgkinson Street, Dromana. Tel: (03) 5986 2974.

Spiritualist Foundation of Victoria, High Street, Armadale. Tel: (03) 9560 3129.

Spiritualist Chapel of Peace and Harmony, 2 Synnot Street, Werribee. Tel: (04) 1110

6491.
Spiritualist Research Society, Gladys Machin Senior Cititzens Club, 8-10 Cedar Street, South Caulfield. Tel: (03) 9571 8806.
Temple Of Truth And Light, 72 Cumberland Road, Pascoe Vale, 3044. Tel: (03) 9740 7037.
The Aquarian Spiritual Awareness Centre, Berwick. Tel: (03) 9720 4402.
Tumbetin Spiritual Centre, 10 Hughes Street, Upwey, 3158, P.O. Box 209, Belgrave, 3160. Tel: (03) 9754 7167.
Victorian Spiritualists Union Inc, 71-73 A' Beckett St., Melbourne, 3000. Tel: (613) 9663 6121.

Western Australia
Alpha Spiritualist Centre, Flinders Community Centre, Broadbeach Bvd. Tel: (09) 9342 4705.
Aquarian Spiritual Centre, 51 Forest Road, Forest Dale. Tel: (09) 397 0155.
Centre Christian Spiritualist Church, 76 Townsend Road, Subiaco, 60. Tel: (08) 9382 3333.
Maylands Christian Spiritualist Church., 123 Caledonian Avenue, Maylands. Tel: (08) 9370 4133.
Melville Spiritualist Centre, Kulungahmyah Family Centre, 136 Le Souf Drive, Kardinya, 61. Tel: (08) 9364 6174.
Melville Spiritualist Centre Inc, Perth. Tel: (09) 364 6174.
Progressive Spiritualist Church, 388 Stirling Street, Highgate, 60. Tel: (08) 9379 1059.
Reality Dreams Spiritual Centre, 31 Coodanup Drive, Mandurah. Tel: (09) 535 4331.
Sacred Flame Spiritualist Church, 12 Watts Road, Safety Bay. Tel: (08) 9419 2209.
SNU Centre of Western Australia, P.O. Box 197, Gosnells, 61.
Spiritualists' National Union of Great Britain. Tel: (08) 9277 8869.

New Zealand
Auckland Christian Spiritualist Church. Tel: (09) 629 0508.
The Spiritualist Alliance (Auckland) Inc, 120 Carlton Gore Road, Newmarket.
Postal Address: P.O. Box 9477, Newmarket, Auckland. Tel: (09) 579 8571.
Church of the Golden Light, 25 New North Road, Auckland.
The New Age Christian Spiritualist Centre, 61 Grafton Street, Christchurch, NZ.
Frontiersman Hall, 61 Dublin Street, Wanganui.

AMERICA
Arizona
Sun Spiritualist Camp Association Inc, 2525 N 355th Avenue, Tonopah. Tel: (602) 386 3877.
The National Spiritualist Summit, 3251 W. Topeka Drive, Glendale, Arizona. Tel: 85308 2325.

Arkansas
Arkansas Spiritual Centre, P.O. Box 290, Ward, Little Rock. Tel: (501) 882 6040.

California

California State Spiritualists Association NSAC, 41 Dearborn Street, San Francisco.

California State Spiritualists' Association, 5537 Whitney Ave, Carmichael, 95608.

Central Spiritualist Church NSAC, 2500 Marconi Avenue 210, Sacramento. Tel: (916) 652 4568.

Chapel of the Angels, 6767 Del Rosa Avenue, San Bernardino, 92. Tel: (909) 887 3011.

Church of Divine Love, 212 Dakota Avenue, Santa Cruz. Tel: (408) 426 2989.

First Christian Spiritualist Church, 1206 Coolidge Avenue, National City. Tel: (619) 477 6424.

First Spiritual Church, 3777 42nd Street, San Diego, 92. Tel: (619) 284 4646.

First Spiritual Temple NSAC, 672 Van Ness (Between 17th & 18th), San Francisco. Tel: (415) 621 0491.

Fraternal Spiritualist Church, 4720 Kensington Drive, San Diego. Tel: (858) 281 4557.

Gate of Heaven Chapel, 21st Century Family Church, 2019 Orange Ave, Ramona, CA. Tel: (818) 343 5030.

Golden Gate Spiritualist Church, 1901 Franklin Street, San Francisco, CA. Tel: (415) 885 9976.

Golden Light of Christ, 11828 Rancho Bernardo Rd, 123-201, San Diego, CA. Tel: (858) 480 5740.

Harmony Grove Spiritualist Association, 2975 Washington Circle, Escondido, CA, 92. Tel: (760) 745 9176.

Harmony Grove Spiritualist Association, 2975 Washington Circle, Escondido, 92029,

HGSA Office. Tel: (760) 745 9176. Fax: (760) 745 3482.

Light of Emmanuel Church, 2558 Erskine Lane, Hayward, CA, 94. Tel: (510) 887 1621.

Light of Truth Church, 564 Bear Valley Parkway, Escondido, CA, 92. Tel: (619) 489 6655.

Missionary Independent Spiritual Church, 6632 Covey Road, Forestville, CA, 95. Tel: (707) 887 1524. Fax: (707) 887 7128.

Mystical United Spiritualist Church, 1212 E. Lincoln Avenue, Anaheim, 92. Tel: (714) 758 8097.

Redwood Church of Spiritual Science, 149 Clinton Street, Redwood, 94. Tel: (415) 598 0111.

San Francisco Spiritualist Society, 1832 Buchanan, California.

Spiritual Centre of Friendship, 125 East G Street, Ontario, CA. Tel: (909) 986 2050.

Spiritual Light Church, 1606 State Street, San Diego, CA, 92. Tel: (858) 273 1311.

Spiritual Science Church, 533 Crane Avenue, Turlock CA. Tel: (209) 669 6128.

Spiritual Science of Life Church NSAC, 729 Morse Street, San Jose, CA, 95. Tel: (209) 293 4795.

Spiritualist Chapel of the Pines, 457 Grass Valley Highway, 19 Auburn, CA, 95. Tel: (916) 823 1816.

Spiritualist Church of Revelation, 200 West Colorado Boulevard, Monrovia, CA, 91. Tel: (626) 256 3403.

Spiritualist Church of Two Worlds NSAC, 1550 San Leandro Boulevard, San Leandro. Tel: (925) 930 6663.

Spiritualist Gathering, 3212 E. Eighth Street, Long Beach, 90. Tel: (562) 861 6158.

St. Andrew's Spiritualist Church, 2936 Rawson Street, Oakland, CA, 94. Tel: (510)

534 5060.
Summerland Spiritualist Church, 1028 Garden Street, Santa Barbara, CA, 93. Tel: (805) 965 4474.
Sunflower Spiritualist Church, 3639 M.L.K. Junior Way, Oakland, CA, 94. Tel: (510) 658 4506.
Temple of Spiritual Truth NSAC, 732 North Sierra Way, San Bernardino, CA, 92. Tel: (909) 825 6809.
United Friendship Christian Spiritualist Church, 812 N Alvarodo, Los Angeles, 90. Tel: (213) 389 9197.
Universal Church of the Master, 501 Washington Street, Santa Clara, CA, 95. Tel: (408) 248 3624.

Colorado
Chapel of Spiritual Awareness, Forte Academy of Music, 10143 W Chatfield Avenue, Suite 15, Littleton, CO, 80. Tel: (303) 797 7227.
Chapel of Spiritual Awareness NSAC, 1939 South Monroe Street, Denver, CO, 80210. Tel: (303) 794 3154.

Connecticut
Albertson Memorial Church, 293 Sound Beach Avenue, Old Greenwich, CT, 06. Tel: (203) 637 4615.
Church of the Infinite Spirit, 80 Walsh Avenue, Newington, CT, 06. Tel: (860) 582 7385.
Connecticut State Spiritualist Association, 101 Leffingwell Avenue, Waterbury, 06710.
First Spiritualist Church of Willimantic, 268 High Street, Willimantic, CT, 06. Tel: (860) 742 7846.
Gifts Of The Spirit, 1595 Route 85, Chesterfield, CT, 06. Tel: (860) 443 3201.
National Spiritualist Church of Norwich Inc., 29 Park Street, Norwich, CT, 06. Tel: (860) 886 8522.
New London Spiritualist Church. Tel: (860) 701 1355.

Florida
Divine Pathways Metaphysical Church, The Cares Enrichment Centre, 12417 Clocktower Parkway, Hudson, FL, 34. Tel: (727) 967 9298.
Celestial Visions School of Metaphysical Arts, 1451 W. Cypress Creek Road, Fort Lauderdale FL, 33. Tel: (954) 928 2845.
Centre of Light, UCM 796, 1517 Hillcrest Street, Orlando, FL, 32. Tel: (407) 228 0101.
Church of Light, 105 West Marion Avenue, Punta Gorda, FL, 33. Tel: (941) 505 1555.
Church of Light, 220 41 Avenue East, Bradenton, FL, 34. Tel: (941) 748 LOVE.
Church of Spiritual Awakening AFSC, Inc., 2978 Old Dixie Highway, Suite E, Kissimmee, Florida. Tel: (407) 851 6510.
Colby Memorial Temple, 1325 Stevens Street, P.O. Box 319, Cassadaga, FL, 32. Tel: (386) 228 3171.
Haven for Spiritual Travellers, 1341 SW 25th Avenue, Fort Lauderdale, FL, 33. Phone: (954) 792 3866.
Healing Light Spiritualist Church, 990 Sunridge Drive, Sarasota, Florida. Tel: (941)

359 5260.

Holiday Metaphysical Church, 5811 Auld Lane, Holiday, FL, 34. Tel: (813) 376 0732.

Spiritual Chapel of Melbourne, 1924 Melody Way, Melbourne, Florida. Tel: (321) 733 1555.

Spiritualist Church of Awareness NSAC, 3210 North Chickasaw Trail, Orlando, 32. Tel: (407) 826 0807.

Spiritualist Church of Melbourne, 2185 Meadowlane Avenue, West Melbourne, FL. Tel: (321) 733 1555.

Spiritual Lighthouse Church, 1049 Crestwood Street, Jacksonville FL, 32. Tel: (904) 764 7639.

St. Andrew's Church of Metaphysics, Inc., 6245 Fletcher Street, Hollywood, FL, 33. Tel: (305) 987 6657.

The Cosmic Church Of Truth, Inc., 1637 Hamilton Street, Jacksonville, 32. Tel: (904) 984 7268.

The Institute for Spiritual Development, 5419 Sherier Place NW, Washington, DC, 20. Tel: (202) 362 2456.

Georgia

National Divine Spiritual Church, 18 Jackson Street, NE Atlanta, GA, 30312. Tel: (404) 522 9153.

Temple Of Inner Peace, P.O. Box 1537, Stone Mountain, GA, 30086. Tel: (404) 299 8705.

Hawaii

Honolulu Church of Light, 1539 Kapiolani Blvd, Honolulu, Hawaii 96814, USA. Tel: (808) 952 0880.

Idaho

Sanctuary for the Spirit, 2660 East Franklin Road, Meridian, 83704. Tel: (208) 888 2088.

Illinois

Cherry Valley Spiritualist Camp Inc., 8002 Service Road, Cherry Valley, IL, 61016. Tel: (815) 332 5359.

Christabelle Spiritualist Church of Aurora Inc., 1204 Game Farm Road, Yorkville, IL, 60560. Tel: (630) 553 2517.

Church of the Spirit, 2651 North Central Park Avenue, Chicago, IL, 60647-01101. Tel: (312) 489 5422.

Crumbaugh JT&EJ Spiritualist Church, 102 South Pearl Street, LeRoy, IL, 61752. Tel: (309) 962 9076.

First Universal Spiritualist Church, Streator, Illinois. Tel: (815) 672 1608.

Puritan Spiritualist Church, 13906 Greenbay Avenue, Burnham, IL, 60633. Tel: (708) 389 5374.

Silent Prayer Sanctuary, 7349 N Addison Street, Chicago, IL, 60634. Tel: (312) 889 7864.

Spiritualist Church of Truth, 6343 West Cuyler, (nr Irving Park), Chicago, IL, 60634. Tel: (708) 452 8754.

Tucker Smith Washington Spiritualist Church, 6146 South Ashland Avenue, Chicago,

IL, 60636. Tel: (312) 436 0366.

Indiana

Aquarian Ministry Ltd, 321 South Ninth Street, Terre Haute, IN, 47802. Tel: (812) 234 5276.

First Spiritualist Church of Gary, 2430 West 11th Avenue, Gary, IN, 46404. Tel: (219) 885 0091.

First Spiritualist Science Church NSAC, 519 South Leeds Avenue, Indianapolis. Tel: (317)291 0799.

Indiana Association of Spiritualists, P.O. Box 132, Chesterfield, IN, 46017. Tel: (317) 378 0235.

Metaphysical Ministries, 1120 6th Avenue, Terre Haute, IN, 47807. Tel: (812) 232 5758.

New Dawn Spirit of Light Church NSAC, 3637 West 10th Street, Indianapolis. Tel: (317) 291 0799.

Progressive Spiritualist Church NSAC, 6225 North Carrollton Avenue, Indianapolis, IN, 46220. Tel: (317) 255 4902.

Psychic Science Spiritual Church, 1415 Central Avenue, IN, 46202. Tel: (317) 634 1430.

Spiritual Science Church NSAC, 314 West Coolspring Avenue, Michigan City, IN, 46360. Tel: (219) 874 002.

Universal Institute for Holistic Studies, Muncie, IN, 47304. Tel: (765) 282 8800.

Universal Worship Centre, 1317 West Wayne Street, Fort Wayne, IN, 46802. Tel: (219) 422 3858.

Iowa

First Spiritualist Church, 5416 6th Avenue South, Clinton. Tel: (319) 243 3233.

Spiritualist Harmony Church, 1429 West Seventh Street, Davenport, IA, 52802. Tel: (319) 324 9659.

Kansas

Meta-Life Light Centre, 226 North Main, Lindsborg. Tel: (785) 227 3716.

Sunet Spiritualist Church, Wells. Tel: (785) 227 9958.

Louisiana

Blessed Mother of Charity Outreach Ministry, 2424 Eads Street, New Orleans. Tel: (504) 947 1695.

Christian Sunlight Spiritual Mission, 422 N Prieur, New Orleans. Tel: (504) 522 3942.

Emanuel Spiritual Church, 2940 Cambronne, New Orleans. Tel: (504) 866 6672.

Evening Star Spiritual Church, 6419 N Robertson, New Orleans. Tel: (504) 277 7891.

God Prince of Protection Spiritual Church, 1301 S Derbigny, New Orleans. Tel: (504) 524 5894.

Israelite Divine Spiritual Church, 3000 Frenchmen, New Orleans. Tel: (504) 947 8397.

Metaphysical Centre, 420 Sutter Street, San Francisco.

Miracle Temple Divine Spiritual Church of Deliverance, 2035 Arizona Street, Baton

170

Rouge, Louisiana 70802. Tel: (225) 383 0352.

Mount Pleasant Spiritual Church of Christ, 3423 Clouet, New Orleans. Tel: (504) 947 3348.

St Anthony Divine Spiritual Temple of Christ, 3019 Live Oak, New Orleans. Tel: (504) 486 3387.

St Paul Spiritual Divine Church of Christ, 3320 Washington, New Orleans. Tel: (504) 821 2059.

St Philip Divine Spiritual Church, 10188 Hyacinth Avenue, Baton Rouge, 70809. Tel: (225) 336 9521.

Watson Memorial Spiritual Temple of Christ, 3619 1st, New Orleans. Tel: (504) 827 1565.

Maine

Clearwater Spiritualist Church Inc., Dover-Foxcroft. Tel: (207) 327 4690,

Etna Spiritualist Camp, Camp Etna, P.O. Box E, Etna, ME, 04434. Tel: (207) 269 2094.

Harrison D. Barrett Spiritualist Church, 114-118 Harlow Street, Bangor, ME, 04078. Tel: (207) 848 2273.

Madison Spiritualist Camp Meeting Association Inc., 74 Central Avenue, Waterville, ME, 04901. Tel: (207) 877 2204.

Maine State Spiritualist Association, 715 Newburgh Road, Hermon, ME. 04401. Tel: (207) 848 2273 or (207) 655 6673.

Pinpoint of Light Spiritualist Centre, Camp Road, Hartford. Tel: (207) 597 2600.

Portland Spiritualist Church, 719 Main Street, Westbrook. Tel: (207) 655 6673.

Maryland

Chapel of the Living Presence, Hampstead. Tel: (410) 239 8624.

The Light Centre Spiritualist Church, The Hampton Inn, 6617 Governor Ritchie Highway, Glen Burnie, MD, 21061. Tel: (410) 590 9167.

Massachusetts

A Place of Light, 374 Main Street, 01. Tel: (508) 892 8928.

First Spiritual Temple, 16 Monmouth Street, Brookline, MA, 02146-5606. Tel: (617) 566 7639.

First Spiritualist Church of Brockton, AGAWAN Grange Hall, 243 Winthrop Street, Route 44, Rehobeth, MA. Tel: (404) 245 8307.

First Spiritualist Church of Onset, Box 231, Onset, MA, 02558. Tel: (508) 295 1085.

First Spiritualist Church of Quincy, 40 West Street, Quincy, MA, 02169. Tel: (617) 770 2246.

First Spiritualist Church of Salem, 34 Warren Street, Salem, MA 01970. Tel: (978) 745 2098.

First Spiritualist Church of Springfield Inc., 33-37 Bliss Street, Springfield, MA 01105. Tel: (413) 732 1234.

Greater Boston Church of Spiritualism, 32 Church Street, Watertown, MA, 02472. Tel: (617) 923 4334.

Medford Spiritualist Church NSAC, 147 High Street, Medford, MA 01970. Tel: (978) 744 0546.

National Spiritualist Alliance of the USA, 2 Montague Avenue, P.O. Box 88 , Lake Pleasant, MA, 01347. Tel: (413) 367 0138.

Plymouth Spiritualist Church, 131 Standish Ave, Plymouth. Tel: (508) 888 6049.
Swampscott Church of Spiritualism, 59 Burrill Street, Swampscott, MA. Tel: (781) 595 6972.

Michigan

Chain Lake Spiritualist Camp Association, 8000 W Chain Lake Road, South Branch, MI 48761. Tel: (517) 257 4133.

Church of Divine Light, 226 E Leonard Street NE. Tel: (616) 451 9788.

Church of Spiritual Truth, P.O. Box 262, Union City, MI 49094. Tel: (517) 278 6733.

Divine Dimensions Institute & Spiritualist Church, 7097 17 Mile Road, Suite 300, Clinton Twp, MI 48038. Tel: (810) 263 4021.

First Psychic Church of Brightmoore, 21729 Fenkell Avenue, Detroit, MI, 48223. Tel: (313) 255 1575.

First Spiritual Church, 906 N Chilson Street, Bay City, MI 48706. Tel: (517) 686 6300.

First Spiritual Temple, 3224 Greenfield Road, Royal Oak, MI 48073. Tel: (248) 548 2240.

Flint Spiritualist Church, 2084 E Judd Road, Burton, MI. Tel: (810) 742 2312.

Flower Memorial Spiritualist Church, 430 West Bellevue Street, Leslie, MI. Tel: (517) 694 8107.

Golden Light Spiritualist Church, Highland Senior Centre, 209 N John Street. Tel: (517) 244 1810.

Golden Rule Spiritualist Church, 07444 Old 31N, Charlevoix, MI 49755. Tel: (231) 537 2938.

Metaphysical Church of Christ, 230 S Holmes Street, Lansing, MI 48912.. Tel: (517) 484 2360.

Metaphysical Church of Prophecy, 3320 Thompson Ave., Muskegon, MI 49441. Tel: (616) 755 1506.

Northern Lake Michigan Spiritualist Camp, 07444 Old 31N, Charlevoix, MI 49755. Tel: (231) 537 2938.

Snowflake Spiritualist Camp, 7750 Snowflake Rd., Bellaire, MI, 49615. Tel: (616) 544 8759.

Spirit of Harmony Chapel NSAC, 340 North Lapeer Road, Oxford, MI 48371. Tel: (810) 814 9172.

Spirit of Harmony Chapel NSAC, 504 Worthington Drive, Oxford, MI, 48371. Tel: (810) 628 2353.

Spiritual Development Chapel, 300 W. Napier Ave., Benton Harbor, MI, 49022. Tel: (616) 927 4333.

Spiritual Episcopal Church, 141 Frost Street, Eaton Rapids, MI 48827. Tel: (517) 663 8460.

Spiritual Episcopal Church, 6577 Garden Drive, 48458, Mt. Morris. Tel: (810) 686 9350.

Spiritual Episcopal Church, Ovid, MI. Tel: (989) 834 2578.

Spiritual Episcopal Church, 610 Clinton Street 48867, Owosso, MI. Tel: (989) 729 9757.

Spiritualist Church of the Good Samaritan, 5401 Oak Park, Clarkston, MI, 48346. Tel: (248) 673 5445.

Spiritualist First Church of Truth, 127 Meerse Street, SE Grand Rapids, MI. Tel: (616) 241 3387.

The First Spiritualist Church of Lansing, 611 Samantha Street, Lansing MI, 48911. Tel: (517) 882 5188.

Minnesota

First Spiritualist Church, 1414 East Ninth Street, Duluth, MN, 55805. Tel: (218) 724 6554.

Second Spiritualist Church, 2230 Lyndale Avenue North, Minneapolis, MN. Tel: (612) 529 0781.

Spirit of Life Spiritualist Church, Lake Harriet Community Building, 4401 Upton Avenue South, Minneapolis, MN 55410. Tel: (763) 535 2746.

Spiritual Episcopal Church, 1119 East Lake Street, Minneapolis, MN 55407. Tel: (612) 735 7478.

Spiritual Science Church, 411 Main Street, St. Paul, MN 55102. Tel: (612) 255 4609.

Third Spirit of Life Spiritualist Church, Unity Church Building, 911 11th Avenue NW, Rochester, MN. Tel: (501) 288 7239.

Missouri

Church of Inner Faith in Christ, 437 So. Cypress, K.C., MO, 64124. Tel: (816) 241 0512.

Fifth Spiritualist Church of St Louis, 6026 South Kingshighway Boulevard, St Louis, MO, 63109. Tel: (314) 353 4779.

Light of the World Spiritualist Chapel, 3724 Red Bridge Road, Kansas City, MO. Tel: (816) 525 0902.

Precious Lord Church, 580 Humes Lane, Florissant, MO. Tel: (314) 838 2336.

United Christian SPL Church, 415 Prospect, KC, MO, 64124. Tel: (816) 241 9546.

Montana

Spiritualist Church of Inner Light, 928 Broadwater Avenue, Billings, MT 59101. Tel: (406) 628 5711.

Nebraska

Spiritual Science & Philosophy Church NSAC, 321 Hascall Street, Omaha, NE 68108-2121. Tel: (402) 345 0101.

Nevada

Spiritualist Church of Eternal Light, 3430 E Tropicana (Trop. Plaza), Ste 62, Las Vegas, NV, 89121. Tel: (702) 362 6184.

Spiritualist Desert Church NSAC, 3355 West Spring Mountain Road, Suite 19, Las Vegas, NV, 89102. Tel: (702) 876 8783.

New Hampshire

The Church of Spiritual Life Inc, Masonic Hall, 109 Main Street, Salem, NH.

New Jersey

Journey Within Spiritualist Church, 2190 Hamburg Turnpike, Wayne, NJ, 07470. Tel: (973) 616 9685.

The Journey Within (SNU Kindred Body/Affiliated), P.O. Box 1413, Clifton, New

Jersey, 07015.

New York

Church of Compassion, 1191 Cornell Ave., Hillcrest, Binghamton, NY, 13901. Tel: (607) 722 2670.
First Spiritualist Temple, 29 Temple Place, East Aurora, NY, 14052. Tel: (716) 652 5018.
First Universal Spiritualist Church of NYC, 208 W 30th Street, Suite 201, 2nd Floor, off 7th Avenue, Manhattan. Tel: (212) 877 6937.
Holistic Studies Institute of New York, 1500 Central Avenue Albany, NY, 12205. Tel: (518) 464 9624.
International Mediumship Institute, 250 W 49th Street, Suite 503, NY, 10. Tel: (877) 375 2873 or (645) 485 9345.
Lily Dale Spiritualist Church, P.O. Box 1128, Lily Dale, NY, 14752.
National Spiritualist Association of Churches, P.O. Box 217, Lily Dale, NY, 14752-0217.
New Horizons Spiritualist Church Inc., 1130 North Broadway, North Masapequa, NY. Tel: (631) 736 1058.
Plymouth Spiritualist Church, Days Inn, 384 East Avenue, Rochester, NY, 14607. Tel: (716) 234 2362.
Plymouth Spiritualist Church, 29 Vick Park, Rochester, 14. Tel: (585) 271 1470.
Sanctuary of Infinite Spirit Inc NSAC, 34 River Road, Smithtown, NY. Tel: (631) 588 3150.
Spiritualist Church of Love and Light, 2141 Eastern Parkway, 2nd Floor Rear, Schenectady, 12. Tel: (518) 372 9280.
Spiritualist Open Centre, 1471 Route 9, Rome Plaza, Clifton Park, NY, 12065. Tel: (518) 383 1931.
Temple of Divine Guidance, 37 Hart St., Albany, NY 11206. Tel: (718) 282 8542.
United Spiritualists' Church, 1600 Broadway, Room 504, NYC, 10019. Tel: (212) 245 4566.
Universal Centre of New Age Consciousness, Queens, NY. Tel: (718) 279 1030.

North Carolina

Asheville First Spiritualist Church, 159 Hillside St, Asheville, NC 2880. Tel: (704) 253 3837.
Church of the Trees, 11629 Kennewick Rd, Charlotte, NC 28216. Tel: (704) 399 5036.

Ohio

Church of Two Worlds NSAC, 2272 Newgate Avenue, 45420. Tel: (513) 256 2129.
Church of Universal Spirit, Mentor, OH, 44060. Tel: (440) 255 1169.
First Spiritualist Church, 4230 Main Avenue, Ashtabula, OH. Tel: (440) 293 7056.
First Spiritualist Church, 636 Western Avenue, Toledo, OH, 43609. Tel: (419) 246 5389.
First Spiritualist Church of Linden, 1751 Aberdeen Avenue, Columbus, OH, 43211. Tel: (614) 263 1631.
Friends Temple of Spiritual Truth, 1555 Laird Drive Ashtabula, OH, 44004. Tel: (440) 964 7461.

IGAS Healing & Learning Centre, 5403 South Ridge West, Ashtabula, OH, 44004. Tel: (440) 969 1724.

Memorial Spiritual Church, 19204 Pawnee Avenue, Cleveland, OH, 44123. Tel: (216) 692 7291.

Memorial Spiritualist Church, 667 Henry Street, Marion, OH, 43302. Tel: (614) 387 8877.

Ohio State Spiritualist Association, P.O. Box 253, Ashley, OH, 43003. Tel: (614) 747 2688.

Rays of Light Spiritualist Church, 82 North High Street, Gahanna, 43. Tel: (614) 268 2894.

Spirit of Love Church, 33 East Cassilly Street, Springfield, OH, 45504. Tel: (937) 325 7381.

Spiritual Life Centre NSAC, 609 Waterliet Avenue, Dayton, OH, 45420. Tel: (937) 878 1165.

Spiritualist Church of Light & Hope, 1401 East McMillan Street, Cincinnati, OH, 45206. Tel: (513) 574 3760.

Spiritualist Church of the Angels, 12550 Chillicothe Road, (Rt 306), Chesterland, 44. Tel: (440) 729 7353.

United Spiritualists of the Christ Light, 128 East Broadway, 45140. Tel: (513) 683 4926.

United Worship Centre, Cleveland, OH. Tel: (800) 229 4224.

Oklahoma

Central Spiritualist Church, 2348 NW 36th Street, Oklahoma City. Tel: (405) 732 7975.

Tulsa Spiritual Centre, 2520 E Admiral Court. Tel: (918) 838 0092.

Oregon

Alice Street Spiritualist Church, 3446 SW Alice Street, Portland. Tel: (503) 246 7300.

New Era Church, 10244 S New Era Road, Canby. Tel: (503) 266 9701.

Spirit Guided Friends Church, 5729 SE Boise Street, Portland, 97. Tel: (503) 771 8986.

Pennsylvania

Christian Spiritualist Church, 461 East 6th Street, Erie, 16. Tel: (814) 459 3795.

First Spiritualist Church of McKeesport, 809 Locust Street, McKeesport. Tel: (412) 672 1272.

Getter Memorial NSAC, 1123 Oak Street, Allentown. Tel: (610) 770 7560.

Greater World Christian Spiritualist Church, 151 E Roosevelt Boulevard, Philadelphia.

Ministry of the Spirit, 12 East 9th Street, Erie. Tel: (814) 490 6498.

Second Spiritualist Church, 423 South Broad Street, Philadelphia, 19. Tel: (215) 735 9630.

St John's Church of Faith, 6th and Washington Street, Allentown. Tel: (610) 791 2641.

Texas

Angels of Light Spiritualist Church NASC, 2714 FM 713 (McMahan Road), Lockhart. Tel: (512) 376 5310.

First Church of Divine Science, 2115 Turner Street, Houston. Phone: (281) 695 2550.

First Spiritualist Church, 802 South College Avenue, P.O. Box 1152, Cameron. Tel: (512) 447 2188.

First Spiritualist Church of Austin, 4200 Avenue D, Austin. Tel: (512) 458 3897.

Louise Scholtz Memorial Chapel NSAC, 1627 Pan Am Express Way North, San Antonia. Tel: (210) 225 2354.

Second Spiritualist Church of Dallas, 13610 Midway Road 212, Dallas. Tel: (972) 675 2303.

Second Spiritualist Church of Dallas NSAC, 1221 Willow Creek Drive, Lancaster, 75. Tel: (972) 218 7772.

Spiritual Science Church, ESP Lab of Texas, 804 E High St, Wills Point. Tel: (903) 896 1700.

White Corral Ranch, Rt 1, Box 370, Hico, 76. Tel: (817) 965 227.

Vermont

Circle of Light Church, O'Brien Civic Centre, Patchen Road, South Burlington, VA. Tel: (802) 879 0045.

Vision of Light Church, 100 Main Street, P.O. Box 133, Windsor, Vermont. Tel: (603) 632 7883.

Virginia

Centre for Spiritual Enlightenment NSAC, 222 North Washington Street, Falls Church. Tel: (703) 645 8060.

Memorial Spiritualist Church NSAC, 307 West 37th Street, Norfolk. Tel: (757) 622 5070.

Washington

Church of Two Worlds NSAC, 3038 Q Street NW Georgetown, 20. Tel: (202) 333 5114.

First Spiritualist Church of Puyallup, 341 2nd Street SE, Puyallup, 98. Tel: (253) 845 4444 or (253) 539 5895.

West Virginia

Camp Edgewood NSAC, 1228 26th Avenue Court, Milton, 98. Tel: (253) 927 2050.

Church of Divine Grace NSAC, 216 1st Avenue, Kent. Tel: (206) 824 7454.

Church of Spiritual Unity NSAC, 1228 26th Avenue Court, Milton. Tel: (206) 927 2365.

Church of Spiritual Unity NSAC, 1228 26th Avenue Court, Milton. Tel: (206) 927 2365.

First Spiritualist Association, Way Memorial Temple, North Broadway Street & Maryland Street, Wheeling Island. Tel: (304) 233 5065.

Institute For Spiritual Development, 5419 Sherier Place, 20016. Tel: (202) 362 2456.

Wisconsin

Church of Spiritual Light, 7336 St. James Street, Wauwatosa, 53. Tel: (414) 453 1975.

First Spiritualist Church of West Allis, 6228 West Washington Street, West Allis, 53. Tel: (414) 545 7650.
Morris Pratt Institute, 11811 Watertown Plank Road, Milwaukee, 53226-3342. Tel: (414) 774 2994.
Western Wisconsin Camp Association NSAC, 304 Hill St., 53968, Wonewoc. Tel: (608) 464 7770.

Canada

Britten Memorial Church Of Canada, 657 Lansdowne Avenue, Toronto, Ontario, M6. Tel: (416) 532 1197.
Burlington Spiritualist Temple (Branch of Christian Spiritual Ministries),
c/o St. Paul's Presbyterian Church, 2600 Headon Forest Drive, Burlington, Ontario. Tel: (905) 525 7947.
London Spiritualist Church, 80 Rectory Street, London, Ontario, Canada, N5Z 1Z8. Tel: (519) 951 0890.
North Burnaby Christian Spiritualist Church, 7804 17th Avenue, Burnaby, BC, V3N 1MZ.
St John's Spiritual Centre, P.O. Box 947. Nelson, BC, Canada, V1. Tel: (250) 825 0193.
The Nanaimo Christian Spiritualist Centre, 71 Caledonia Avenue, Nanaimo BC, Canada.
Toronto Spiritualist Temple, 706 College Street, Toronto, Ontario, M6. Tel: (416) 535 2204 Toll Free: 1 866 40.

NOTES

NOTES

NOTES

NOTES

NOTES

NOTES

www.apexpublishing.co.uk

Printed in the USA
CPSIA information can be obtained
at www.ICGtesting.com
LVHW031400250224
772732LV00002B/406